VOLUNTEER RECRUITMENT, INTERVIEWING, AND PLACEMENT

Marlene Wilson, General Editor

Group's Volunteer Leadership Series™
Volume 4
Group's Church Volunteer Central™

Loveland, Colorado

Group's Volunteer Leadership Series™, Volume 4

Volunteer Recruitment, Interviewing, and Placement

Visit our Web site: **www.grouppublishing.com**

Credits
Writer: Mikal Keefer
Editor: Mikal Keefer
General Editor: Marlene Wilson
Chief Creative Officer: Joani Schultz
Art Director: Nathan Hindman
Cover Designer: Jeff Storm
Production Manager: Peggy Naylor

Unless otherwise noted, Scripture taken from the HOLY BIBLE, NEW INTERNATIONAL
VERSION®. Copyright © 1973, 1978, 1984 International Bible Society. Used by permission
of Zondervan Publishing House. All rights reserved.

Produced with the assistance of The Livingstone Corporation
(www.LivingstoneCorp.com). Project staff includes Chris Hudson, Ashley Taylor, Mary
Horner Collins, Joel Bartlett, Cheryl Dunlop, Mary Larsen, and Rosalie Krusemark.

Library of Congress Cataloging-in-Publication Data

Volunteer recruitment, interviewing, and placement / Marlene Wilson, general
        editor.—1st American hardbound ed.
    p. cm. — (Group's volunteer leadership
    series ; v. 4)
    ISBN 0-7644-2748-2 (alk. paper)
    1. Voluntarism—Religious aspects—Christianity. 2. Christian leadership. 3.
Church work. 4. Volunteers—Recruiting. I. Wilson, Marlene. II. Series.
BR115.V64V655 2003
253'.7—dc22   2003022121

10 9 8 7 6 5 4 3 2 1   12 11 10 09 08 07 06 05 04

Printed in the United States of America.

Contents

Introduction

Take a look at these four recruitment techniques. If they look familiar, you're in trouble . . .

When it comes to recruiting volunteers, there's a long list of ideas that simply don't work. Maybe you've tried one of these . . .

- You have the pastor hold the Sunday morning service hostage until someone signs up for nursery duty next week.

- You place inserts in the Sunday morning bulletins week after week after week until you get enough names to staff the Sunday school.

- You stand the cutest little girl you can find up front in the worship service asking for someone—*anyone*—to come help her understand Jesus. Extra points if her lower lip is quivering and there's a single tear creeping slowly down one cheek.

- You send letters home with all the fourth-grade boys demanding their parents take turns serving as helpers—or else. It's not until later you realize all the letters wound up as ammunition in a paper wad fight out in the parking lot.

It's no surprise that those techniques of volunteer recruitment are destined to fail. Anyone who's made a compelling announcement asking for volunteers and then stood at a lonely sign-up table suspects there *must* be a better way.

There is.

The remainder of this Volunteer Leadership Series will help you create a volunteer ministry that makes use of the best possible recruitment techniques. You'll learn new, proven approaches to getting the right people in the right spots. You'll gain new skills that make recruitment easier. You'll learn to think about volunteers and managing volunteers in a new way.

And your new way of thinking begins here. It starts with a new definition of what it means to "recruit" a volunteer.

ONE

Recruitment Redefined

A new way of thinking about recruitment. Trends in volunteerism. Why people do—and don't—volunteer. And what *really* motivates volunteers.

Many people think that recruiting volunteers is a matter of crafting a sales message and then putting the people who respond to work. We tuck those warm bodies into open volunteer slots and then move on.

The problem with that approach is that volunteers who enter a ministry that way don't stick. They aren't fulfilled and they usually aren't effective. You end up right back on the same old treadmill, trying to replace people who you got to replace other people who themselves were replacements.

A certain amount of turnover will happen no matter what you do. But you can shrink turnover and increase volunteer satisfaction (yours with the volunteers, and the volunteers with their roles) by thinking of recruitment as *more* than a sales job. And by determining that just any warm body *won't* do for your volunteer ministry.

Think of recruitment this way:

Recruitment is an invitation to come discuss a volunteer role.

It doesn't mean the person responding will necessarily get the job.

Notice that when you recruit with this definition in mind, the process is like a job interview, where a company selects from among a talented pool of applicants. It's not a desperate attempt to get somebody doing a job that needs to be done.

But you might be thinking: *I AM desperately seeking people to do jobs that need to be done! I can't AFFORD to be selective.*

Not only can you afford to be selective, you *must* be selective. To do anything else is to shortchange everyone in the process—the volunteers, your church, and the people who will benefit from the volunteers' involvement.

Consider what happened to a youth minister who was short a youth sponsor and was then introduced to someone who wanted the job . . .

> "You *must*
> be selective."

"The guy looked perfect for the role," says John, the youth minister. "He was good-looking, high energy, and related well with the kids. Plus, I had so many parents telling me he'd make a wonderful youth sponsor that I felt I had to try him out."

Mistake.

After a month of stellar service, the new 25-year-old youth sponsor decided to date one of the senior high girls.

The good news is that John happened to walk into the conversation while the sponsor was telling the girl what time he'd pick her up for their date—so the date never happened.

"I was shocked," says John. "My heart went to my throat, my stomach fell to my feet, and I thought, "am I *hearing* this? I wanted to *kill* the guy."

Nothing on the security screening had indicated the new volunteer abused children. Or sexually molested teenage girls. Or even drove too fast in a school zone. And in fact the volunteer never *had* done any of those things.

"He just met a nice girl and wanted to take her out," remembers John. "When I told him he couldn't date the kids, he was baffled. He didn't see what the problem was. He didn't have a clue."

Would it have been worth John's time to be more selective about whom he placed in the youth sponsor role? Absolutely.

And would he have been smart to sit down with the sponsor and cover the bases about what was—and wasn't—appropriate behavior? You bet.

But John was desperate for staff and wasn't sure he'd do any better if he kept looking. So he took a shortcut and bypassed the orientation and training—something he will no longer do.

"Nothing happened, but it easily could have," says John, who still serves in a position where he's responsible for finding volunteers. "I learned a *lot* from that experience."

When you live in a world of too many jobs and too few volunteers, how can you turn down people who are willing? The harsh reality is this: Sometimes you have to go with the people you have available. The *good* people—the people you *wish* you had—aren't the ones signing up when you pass around the sign-up sheet.

> "How can you turn down people who are willing?"

What's wrong with people these days? Why isn't anyone volunteering anymore?

Trends in Volunteerism

The fact is that people *are* volunteering—just not in the ways you may remember.

Back in the Good Old Days, when relatively few women worked outside the home, you could sign up volunteers by simply announcing a need. Back in the Good Old Days, when the work week was 40 hours long and families played badminton in the backyard after dinner, men had time to get together on Saturday afternoon to do yard work at the church building.

But those Good Old Days are gone—if they ever existed at all.

These days you're facing trends that shape how much time people are willing to volunteer, and how they want their volunteer commitments structured. Your community may differ somewhat, but in general, you'll need to consider these following 12 trends when you're creating your volunteer ministry.

• **Work life is expanding—and varied.**

How many people do you know who still work the hours of 9 to 5, Monday through Friday? Some studies indicate that only about a third of employees work those once-normal hours.

Part-time jobs, jobs that demand travel and long hours, service jobs with irregular hours, health-care jobs that require night shifts, extra jobs, home-based jobs that blur the lines between "family time" and "work time"; these are common today. So are long commutes that consume extra hours each day.

> "People staffing your volunteer roles will be juggling jobs, families, friends, and their volunteer duties."

Many churches want to find people who'll commit for several months at exactly the time many volunteers are seeking short-term, one-shot volunteer assignments.

According to Independent Sector's *Giving and Volunteering in the United States* (Washington, D.C., 1999), 61 percent of persons who are employed part-time volunteer, and 58 percent of persons who work full-time volunteer. That means the majority of people staffing your volunteer roles will be juggling jobs, families, friends, and their volunteer duties.

• **Families are changing.**

In many homes, grandparents are now raising their grandchildren. Single-parent households are far more common than they once were. The traditional definition of "family" is being stretched and redefined in many directions, and there are unique stresses with each definition. Woe be to the organization that assumes stay-at-home moms will sign up to be Den Mothers, recess chaperones, or Sunday school teachers because those moms want to contribute to organizations that benefit children.

- **People seek balanced lives—and that may eliminate volunteering.**

In an effort to live lives that include family, friends, work, and worship, many church members are opting to intentionally *not* volunteer for tasks. This isn't a lack of concern or unawareness. It's a deliberate decision to limit the number of their obligations, and for these potential volunteers a "no" is a non-negotiable "no."

- **There's increased competition for volunteers.**

Organizations that were once well funded by government agencies are experiencing budget reductions. Every organization is trying to do more with less. The demand for volunteer labor is increasing, which means your church members might very well have full volunteer schedules at the United Way, Homeless Shelter, or SPCA before you ever contact them about serving on a church committee.

- **The motivation for volunteering is shifting.**

In the 1950s and before, the value behind volunteering was commitment. When you signed on to teach Sunday school, you did so because you were expressing a commitment to God, the church, and the children.

Today the values behind volunteerism seem to be compassion (I want to help and make a difference) and community (I want to be part of something bigger than myself. I want to belong and to be in a network of caring people).

Motivation impacts *everything* in a volunteer setting, from how you recruit volunteers to how you assign them to how you recognize them.

- **Volunteers expect more.**

Maybe they used to settle for that "good feeling" that came from helping others, but now they're expecting the organizations that use them to be professional, flexible, and responsive. Good enough isn't good enough anymore. If a volunteer experience is disorganized, frustrating, or wastes the volunteer's time, that volunteer won't be back.

- **There's a changing pool of volunteers available.**

As Baby Boomers reach the age of wanting to do something significant in addition to something lucrative, highly trained and highly skilled people are becoming volunteers. The ranks of volunteers are also growing because of layoffs. Teenagers are entering the volunteer pool because of experience with school "service learning" projects and to bolster resumés for college applications and job searches.

- **Volunteers want to shoulder responsibility, not just tasks.**

Many volunteers bring significant management experience with them when they show up to volunteer. They want to be actively engaged in their roles, which means they want to use all of their skills. Electrical engineers won't be satisfied for long stuffing envelopes. Volunteers are seeking meaningful, interesting work.

- **There are more volunteer options available in churches.**

As churches grow in size, the number of "niche" ministries grows. It used to be a volunteer could work in Christian Education or serve on a board. Now a volunteer can help direct traffic, handle finances, play bass in the worship band, or serve coffee in the café.

- **Guilt is gone as a motivator.**

"Because you should" isn't a reason people willingly accept any longer. Rather, volunteers are motivated for other reasons and they're more willing to explicitly ask what benefits will come to them as a result of their volunteering.

Volunteer managers must be able to answer the question "What's in it for me?" with clear, definite benefits that will flow to the volunteer.

- **Technology is changing volunteering.**

It's now possible to write, edit, and produce the church's monthly newsletter without ever setting foot in the church office. Balancing the books requires software, not board meetings. And the list of technology-related volunteer roles—handling lights and sound, computer consulting, and preparing PowerPoint presentations among others—is growing rapidly. Some volunteer positions require specialized knowledge and thorough training.

- **The cost of training and maintaining volunteers is rising.**

It's more expensive than ever to bring a volunteer on board at your church. The cost of a security screening, the training needed to make a volunteer proficient in a role, insurance to protect the church and volunteer—even the paperwork for tracking volunteers is more extensive than ever before.

> "These trends aren't good or bad; they simply exist."

It's unlikely this trend will reverse direction anytime soon, if ever.

Please note that these trends aren't good or bad; they simply exist. They're reality. And as you plan how to initiate a volunteer management ministry or fine-tune the one that's already in place in your church, you've got to keep them in mind. Wishing there were more stay-at-home moms who want to donate a day per week to your project won't make it come true.

Why Won't People Volunteer?

Everyone who's attempted to staff a ministry with volunteers has a top-ten list of excuses they hear again and again. But the items on those lists usually boil down to two basic issues: a perceived lack of time and fear.

The perceived lack of time

Fact: We all get 24 hours in a day, and 168 hours in a week. The amount of time available to volunteers and non-volunteers is precisely the same.

The concern about having enough time to volunteer really isn't about time. It's about the number of obligations a potential volunteer has that make a claim on his or her time.

If a person is pulled in many different directions and rushes through a nonstop hectic schedule, it's going to feel as if there's no time to spare, . . . and there isn't. One unforeseen incident sets off a domino effect that leaves the next ten appointments missed or delayed. There's no margin in this person's life.

For each potential volunteer, there is a critical issue you must settle before you place the volunteer in a role: Will this person dedicate enough time to the role to be successful? And can the volunteer provide the *right* time? Is the volunteer available when the volunteer job needs to be done?

> **"Will this person dedicate enough time to the role to be successful?"**

A busy sales professional decided to join the Big Brothers. Following the necessary interview and screening process, a first meeting was set up to introduce the volunteer to a potential match. An agency representative was present, as was the volunteer, the eight-year-old boy who was seeking a big brother, and the boy's mother.

The agency representative laid out the agency's expectations again. The big and little brother would meet once a week for three to four hours, meetings would be confirmed by phone 24 hours in advance, outings would be inexpensive, and all parties would stay in touch with the agency. Everything was exactly as described in earlier communications with the individual parties.

Then the mother casually mentioned that the meetings would have to be on Mondays between 3:00 and 6:00 P.M. Weekends were already booked with activities and her work schedule was set.

The connection between the boy and volunteer never developed. For the volunteer, Mondays were busy—especially during work hours. He could meet with the boy on weekends and evenings, but not during work hours.

The volunteer experience failed to develop, but *not* because the volunteer lacked time. It failed to develop because the time the volunteer *had available* didn't match the task.

As you seek to match busy people with volunteer roles, what can you do to overcome the barrier of a perceived lack of time?

Some suggestions:

- **Segment volunteer roles so there are more, but less time-consuming, roles to fill.**

For instance, rather than ask a Sunday school teacher to gather supplies, prepare the lesson, and teach the lesson, you might have another volunteer do the gathering of supplies. Divide volunteer roles into contained tasks and recruit more volunteers who each do less.

- **Connect the volunteer role with another valued activity.**

For instance, if a potential volunteer wants to spend more time with family, suggest a volunteer role that can be accomplished by a family. If the potential volunteer wants to get more exercise suggest the volunteer mow a yard, weed a garden, or do another exercise-oriented task.

- **Suggest that the potential volunteer sign up for a one-shot project rather than an ongoing role.**

An airline pilot whose flight schedule won't allow her to consistently lead a small group on Wednesday night might very well be willing to give a full day some weekend when she's off. Sometimes it's not the amount of time that's a problem; it's the expectation that the same hour will be available each week.

Short-term missions are growing in popularity because they're short term—and can be accomplished by someone who's not willing to completely change his or her life. Habitat for Humanity (www.habitat.org) and Group Workcamps (www.groupworkcamps.com) have found ways to recruit thousands of volunteers who do remarkable amounts of ministry in short-term settings.

- **Create flexible volunteer positions that are less time sensitive.**

It doesn't really matter if someone creates a form on your church web site at 9:00 in the morning or at midnight. And if you're planning ahead, stocking up on animal crackers for VBS can happen anytime during the week before VBS begins. Be intentional about structuring volunteer opportunities so they have the maximum time flexibility possible. This won't be possible with some roles—such as leading a class that meets from 9:30 to 10:30 on Sunday mornings, but it will be possible elsewhere.

• **Create volunteer positions that don't require travel.**

Especially for older volunteers who might be homebound or have issues with travel at night or in bad weather, look for volunteer tasks and roles that don't require travel. Some examples: making phone calls, creating follow-up packets for visitors, and creating craft packets from materials delivered to the volunteers' homes.

When "I don't have time" emerges as an issue in dealing with volunteers, don't assume you understand what the potential volunteer means by those words. It's worth probing to see if one of the strategies listed above can manage the issue and make it possible for the potential volunteer to sign up for a role.

Fear of volunteering

Some people shy away from volunteering because of fear. Not necessarily fear of your organization or the specific opportunities you're offering, but rather three other things . . .

• **They're afraid they'll fail.**

If a volunteer role is poorly defined or lacks training and resources, failure is an almost certain outcome. If volunteers sense they're set up for failure, they won't feel excited about participation.

Volunteers dislike crashing and burning on projects, or disappointing themselves and you. It's up to you to design the volunteer role so you can provide reassurance that no volunteer will be sent out on a limb that will then be cut off.

• **They're afraid of being abused.**

Abuse is a strong word and may overstate the case—but not by much. When a volunteer is given an impossible task, it feels like abuse.

Jim Wideman, in his book *Children's Ministry Leadership: The You-Can-Do-It Guide* (Group Publishing, 2003), describes what sometimes happens to people who sign up to teach Sunday school. "In many churches, new Sunday school teachers are trained by getting a little lecture, handed a book, thrown in a classroom, and told to not come out until Jesus returns."

Jim describes what happens to new volunteer teachers this way: "We tell them they'll get some help and in a couple years we *do* find them a helper. That's when we open the classroom door and are amazed when the teacher comes screaming out, quits on the spot, and disappears forever. So what do we do? We hand the book to the helper we found and throw *that* person in the room."

> "When a volunteer is given an impossible task, it feels like abuse."

Small wonder someone in a church like that would be afraid to sign up to teach Sunday school. You can't quit and there's no training. It's a volunteer's nightmare . . . and it's abusive.

A volunteer would only have to be mistreated that way once before deciding: *never again.* And the only way to be *sure* it never again happens would be to avoid all volunteer roles.

By the way: Volunteers consider it equally abusive to take them on and then give them nothing worthwhile to do.

• **They're afraid they're not "good enough."**

On a typical Sunday morning a church member will see someone preach, teach, and lead music. There may be solo instrumentalists, a band, or a choir. There may be people ushering. Perhaps there are greeters and people staffing an information desk.

And depending on the size of the church and the church's emphasis on excellence in programming, the people serving in visible roles might be demonstrating professional-level skills. They're not just singing—they're singing remarkably well. They're not just playing piano—they're playing at a level you'd expect to hear in a concert hall. They're not just ushering, they look like the concierge at the five-star hotel downtown.

The unintended message: If you're going to serve here, you've got to have the skill and polish of a pro. In our choir, only music majors need apply.

Is that true? Probably not . . . or maybe it *is* true.

A church's desire to have excellent programming creates a smoother, more enjoyable worship service. But it also discourages potential volunteers who know they can't hit the high notes or deliver a top-notch lesson. It can seem there's no place for a nonprofessional to participate.

Here are ways you can banish fear when it comes to volunteering:

- **Define roles carefully—with a full job description in writing.**

Job descriptions provide reassurance to potential volunteers in that they know what they're getting into—and you've thought through what you want. Solid information tends to help people see a challenge as an opportunity or adventure rather than a threat.

See volume 3 for information about how to create job descriptions.

- **Listen carefully to concerns about the volunteer role and the volunteer's fit with the role.**

What's behind the concern? Has the volunteer failed in another volunteer role? Has a friend failed in the role you're proposing? Is there a question of trust about how thoroughly you've described what's expected? What history is the potential volunteer carrying into the discussion? If you detect fear or suspicion, gently probe to get to the root of it.

- **Remove uncertainty.**

Volunteers can be less than confident about participating because they know they're being "sold" on a project. Sure, you're here now—when the volunteer hasn't yet been reeled in—but will you be around when there's a problem to be solved?

Let potential volunteers know what you'll do to help them in their volunteer efforts. Describe the support and involvement they can expect from you and other leaders. Then do what you say you'll do.

The Unspoken Barrier to Volunteering

There's another common reason people don't volunteer, though you'll never hear people actually say it: tradition.

In many churches it's a *tradition* to simply sit in the pew. Few people ever volunteer for anything. It's a *tradition* to pay the soloists who sing on Sunday morning, the nursery workers who care for children on Wednesday night, and the caterers who've replaced the potlucks.

Recruiting volunteers in a church culture that doesn't honor or encourage volunteerism is a challenge of Olympian proportions. And at heart, it's a spiritual matter.

> "Another common reason people don't volunteer: tradition."

If you're in a church where volunteering "just isn't done," consider doing the following:

Meet with the leadership.

Determine if your assessment is accurate. Is it true that most people won't volunteer, or is that true just of one ministry area? If the children's ministry area can't beg, borrow, or steal a volunteer but the adult ministry has a waiting list for involvement, the problem may be with the reputation or administration of the children's ministry area. Be sure you see things clearly, and that you're fixing the right problem.

And if most members of your congregation *are* volunteering in service but only outside your church, that's helpful to know.

Ask leadership to provide teaching about the biblical expectation for involvement.

If people truly aren't serving anywhere, ask for clear teaching about the biblical mandate to serve others. Volume 1 of this series will provide your leadership an excellent starting place for researching that mandate.

Remove every barrier you can find to volunteering.

Some have been identified already, but consider these possibly hidden barriers, too:

- *Do staff members discourage volunteers?* It can be done by failing to design roles that can be filled by volunteers, or refusing to provide information that allows volunteers to function effectively.

- *Is there such competition for volunteers that it frightens volunteers away?* If the new members' class is stalked by the youth pastor, children's pastor, and other staffers who are all pitching the importance of their different ministries, it may create an environment that actually repels volunteerism. To say "yes" to one staffer creates hard feelings with other staffers.

- *Is there a "volunteer toxic" environment that combines a refusal to delegate with vague or nonexistent job descriptions?* It may be so difficult to come on board as a volunteer that it's truly not worth the effort.

- *Are volunteers ignored?* Find out when the last volunteer recognition effort was organized. If the year starts with "19–" then you've identified one problem to overcome.

In volume 1 of this series we identify the common obstacles to volunteerism . . . be sure they're whittled down or cleared out altogether before you start a recruitment campaign.

Pray—and invite others to pray with you.

Is your church one that's discouraged—and as a congregation you have no vision for the future?

Is your church one that's defeated? Perhaps your "glory days" of attendance and impact were 20 or 50 years ago, and those who remain see themselves as defenders of a glorious tradition. Your leadership has dug in and is holding on . . . and that's all.

Is your church dead? There's no spark of life anywhere you look?

Pray for your church and what God wants to do with you. Ask others whose hearts align with yours about wanting to see people involved to join you in regular times of lifting your church up to God.

A bonus: the single best-kept secret of effective recruitment revealed!

There's a simple technique that will revolutionize your recruitment efforts. It's powerful, simple, and you can do it without having to invest in additional books, conferences, or consultants.

And you even get immediate feedback when this technique is used.

Ready?

Here it is: Ask people to serve.

It's that simple. Honest.

> "Ask people to serve."

One of the reasons most frequently cited by volunteers as to why they didn't get involved sooner is that nobody asked them to do so.

That *doesn't* mean they weren't subjected to countless recruitment campaigns. They may have walked past sign-up tables, sat through announcements, and flipped past the pleas for help written in the church newsletter and bulletin.

But nobody *asked* them, face to face, by name, to fill a volunteer role.

If it's increasingly difficult for you to get volunteers, consider how large a role person-to-person recruitment plays in your approach. It is far, *far* more effective than "paper-to-people" recruitment efforts.

What *Really* Motivates Volunteers

First, a disclaimer: You can't motivate a volunteer. It's simply not within your power. But you can discover what already motivates individual volunteers and try to scratch those particular itches.

Everyone has what Marlene Wilson calls a "motivational preference." If you can identify it, you can help each volunteer have a meaningful experience while volunteering through your program.

David McClelland and John W. Atkinson did groundbreaking research at Harvard University and the University of Michigan, respectively, which led to a theory that goes a long way toward helping you identify what motivates your volunteers. A brief listing of their seminal studies is given at the end of this chapter.[1]

Fortunately, Harvard professor George Litwin and his research assistant, Robert Stringer, Jr., helped translate the McClelland-Atkinson theory and applied it to organizations in their book, *Motivation and Organizational Climate.* Marlene Wilson adapted these ideas to working with volunteers in her book, *The Effective Management of Volunteer Programs,* and the following synopsis appears courtesy of Harvard Division of Research, Graduate School of Business and Volunteer Man-agement Associates.

> "A disclaimer: You can't motivate a volunteer."

McClelland and Atkinson were curious about why one person's favorite job was another person's least favorite, and why some people liked to figure things out on their own while others wanted clear directions.

Starting with the premise that "people spend their time thinking about what motivates them," they conducted extensive studies checking out what people thought while walking, eating, working, studying, and even sleeping. They discovered people *do* think about what motivates them, and they identified three distinct motivational types: Achievers, Affiliators, and Power (or Influence) people.

Let's take a closer look at those three motivational types.

Achievers value accomplishments and results.

They like to set goals and solve problems. They want to know where they're headed and want things to happen in a timely way. They *hate* having their time wasted.

Achievers tend to be well-organized, prefer deadlines, are

moderate risk takers, and are often articulate. They like "to-do" lists. They depend on their pocket-calendars and electronic organizers. And if achievers have a leader who's poor at delegation, they'll go crazy.

If an achiever responds to a project they think is significant and they discover it's just a small task, the achiever's motivation immediately deflates. In fact, unless they're extremely committed to the cause, you'll lose them.

In churches resistant to change, where achievers have no room to grow and stretch, you'll find them coming in one door and going out another. You can utilize and attract achievers by learning how to use task forces effectively (see volume 2). Search for achievers with good delegation skills, and they'll form excellent teams around themselves.

Affiliators are "people people."

They're sensitive, nurturing, and caring. Interacting with others and being part of a community is what motivates them. They care less about the work being done than about the people they're doing it with. They're easily hurt, so leaders need to know that affiliators will require more of their time. However, it's time well spent because affiliators make church a good place to be. They're the ones walking up to visitors and striking up conversations.

Affiliators are good barometers about how things are going in your volunteer program. They know how people are feeling about things. They're also good persuaders, listeners, and public speakers. They make excellent interviewers, members of listen-care teams, or leaders of small groups.

And they're great choices for projects like mass mailings. Get a group of affiliators together with a pot of coffee, and they'll have the mailing done before you know it—and enjoy the process because they chatted the entire time.

Power People come in two varieties: McClelland categorized them as *personal* and *social*.

Both types like to think about having impact on people and outcomes. They think long-term and are good strategists.

If you want to enact change, find some power-motivated people and get them on your side. If you convince them, they'll spend their time thinking about who they need to influence and how they need to do it.

Personal Power People use their power on *people,* usually through manipulation and intimidation. They think in terms of win-lose, and if they perceive someone else is "winning," they instantly assume they're losing. They're comfortable with conflict—and tend to create a lot of it!

In the church, these people can be toxic. If someone has left your church bleeding, there was probably a personal power person involved. These are also the people who can quickly crush programs and new ideas.

Social Power People like to influence and impact others in a win-win way. Convince a social power person of your vision, and they'll move mountains to see your project happen. The reason they can do this is because they see power as infinite and self-renewable. The more power they give away, the more they get. Therefore, they aren't threatened by the success of others. Their goal is *your* success. How the church needs these people!

> "In the church, personal power people can be toxic."

By the way, social power people are the best at dealing with personal power people because they aren't intimidated by them. *Never* send an affiliator to deal with a personal power person.

Please understand that most people have some characteristics from each of these motivational types, and an individual's primary motivational style may change over time and within differing situations. Marlene Wilson reports that she has exhibited all three styles.

When she was a homemaker while her children were young, she was an affiliator. When she became a program director, she shifted into achievement. She used to enjoy thinking about program goals, or how to write a book or produce a video series. Now she sees herself as a social power person. She finds herself thinking, *"How do I influence things that matter? How do I use whatever time and energy I have left to have the most impact on the things I care most about?"*

You can motivate people with these three styles by placing them in appropriate settings. For instance, an affiliator may make a wonderful receptionist, so long as the job doesn't also require a great deal of pressure to get filing and typing done on a tight schedule.

And you can use insights drawn from these types to create appropriate recognition for individual volunteers, too. You'll find a detailed list of suggestions in volume 6, on pages 94-95.

1. Seminal studies contributing to this paradigm include: David C. McClelland, *The Achieving Society* (Princeton, NJ: D. Van Nostrand Company, 1961); John W. Atkinson, *An Introduction to Motivation* (Princeton, NJ: D. Van Nostrand Company, 1964); John W. Atkinson and N. T. Feather, *A Theory of Achievement Motivation* (New York: John Wiley and Sons, 1966).

TWO
Marketing Your Volunteer Ministry

How to effectively craft a message and attract people to your volunteer ministry. Ten critical questions. The most effective marketing campaign ever.

Marketing your volunteer ministry simply means this: deliberately telling your target audience the benefits your volunteer ministry can provide to them.

The term "marketing" sometimes has a negative association because it's the same word used to describe how tobacco companies create smokers, whiskey companies create drinkers, and car manufacturers put their super-sized models in garages.

It would seem that in the church, where it's understood that everyone has an ability, interest, or passion to share for the common good, where everyone is called to be active in ministry, and where discipleship is an expectation, there would be no need for "marketing" service opportunities.

> " 'Marketing' sometimes has a negative association."

After all, shouldn't church people be *looking* for volunteer opportunities?

Well . . . yes. But people often *aren't* looking. And if they are, there's lots of competition for the slice of time they have available for volunteering.

If you want to be heard and have people respond, it's important that you target an audience you want to address. Be intentional about crafting a message that cuts through daily clutter and makes an impression.

The best way to be sure that you are effectively communicating with people you want to address is to create a "marketing plan." With a marketing plan, you won't waste time and resources talking to yourself, to the wrong people, or to nobody at all. You'll make the critical decisions up front that will direct how, when, and where you communicate about the volunteer opportunities in your church. You won't find yourself answering the questions a marketing plan addresses when it's a crunch time and you're stressed.

> "You already have the information and resources you need to create a marketing plan."

Here's the good news: You already have the information and resources you need to create a marketing plan. You won't need to go hide out for a month digging through church records, or hire an expensive expert to pull together a serviceable plan. You can do it.

And we'll walk you through the steps.

How to Create a Marketing Plan

First, let's clear up a couple of misunderstandings about marketing.

Marketing is *not* selling.

Marketing is simply a deliberate process of getting your message out to the people you want to hear it in a clear, concise manner.

Marketing is *not* manipulation.

The goal of your communication should never be to somehow trick people into volunteering. That's completely counterproductive. You end up with people you don't want as volunteers, and your volunteer ministry gains a reputation that will keep good people away.

Marketing is *not* just for people with MBAs.

There's nothing terribly complicated about what you'll be

doing, but it will require your making decisions. Since you can't do everything ("Let's take out a full page ad in the newspaper announcing we need nursery workers!"), you've got to decide what you *will* do—and your marketing plan is where you narrow down your communication options.

Marketing is *not* a once-per-year event.

If your church limits marketing and recruiting to a few weeks per year, perhaps as you head into the fall, you're limiting your effectiveness. You need volunteers all year, and people enter your congregation all year. So why wait to put those new people to work?

Plus, if every volunteer position comes up for renewal at the same time, you're almost guaranteeing a training nightmare as you have a large percentage of staff exit and other people come on board.

Finally, remember the wise words shared by an unknown marketing genius: *out of sight, out of mind.* If the volunteer ministry falls off the congregation's radar screen the majority of the year, it will be treated like a temporary distraction—not an integral part of the congregational life.

To create a marketing plan, you must answer ten critical questions. Let's look at these carefully.

1. What is the purpose of your volunteer ministry?

You will want to create a purpose statement, but before you tackle that, be sure you've got a mission statement in place. It's best if you create one in the context of a task force, and you'll find step-by-step help in volume 2 about how to craft a mission statement.

But here's a quick explanation: A mission statement communicates who you are, what you do, what you stand for, and why you do what you do. It's clearly articulated, widely understood, and truly supported by your church leadership, your volunteers, and by you. Your mission statement is the banner you hold up to rally the troops and to let potential volunteers know what you're about.

Before you market your "product" (presumably connecting people with volunteer opportunities and helping people be successful in those opportunities), you've got to be able to describe what you're doing. The clearer you are, the better you'll communicate with your target audience.

Your mission statement is an integral part of your marketing plan. If you *don't* have a mission statement—or the mission statement you have is vague or not compelling—take time to revisit it or to create a statement when you've assembled your task force.

> "The clearer you are, the better you'll communicate."

Your volunteer ministry's *purpose* is tucked away in your mission statement. It's the problem you want to solve, or the thing you want to accomplish. It's the reason you exist as an organization or a ministry.

Some questions that might help you get at your purpose in order to craft a purpose statement are:

- Who does your volunteer ministry serve?

- What services does your volunteer ministry provide to those you serve?

- What is unique about your ministry?

Be sure your purpose clearly identifies why your ministry exists and is inspirational to your paid staff, volunteers, and the people you're serving. A test: Run the purpose statement past your most dedicated volunteers—the ones you wish you could clone. How do they respond to it? Does it capture what motivates them to be involved?

And be sure your purpose statement can keep everyone focused on what's truly important in your ministry.

2. **What can you say—in a "sound bite"—about your volunteer ministry?**

You probably won't be interviewed by a national news network this week, but if you were and you had to sum up what you do in just a few seconds, could you do it?

A "sound bite" is a short statement that captures the spirit of what you're doing in your volunteer ministry. It's a quick, catchy phrase that a news story would run on the air. And it's the sort of phrase that will stick with people who hear about your volunteer ministry.

When creating a sound bite for your marketing, make sure it's brief, catchy, and packed with exciting, descriptive words. Make it memorable, and have it tell the essence of what your ministry does.

These sample sound bites will give you a taste of what you're after:

"Lend an ear, gain a friend."

"Help us grow kids who care."

"Make a friend for life."

"Serve a child, serve the Savior."

There will be many times that you have a brief opportunity to market your volunteer ministry. Be able to do so in ten seconds or less.

Some professional salespeople actually prepare what they call "elevator presentations," brief pitches that can be delivered in an elevator as it travels from the tenth floor to the ground floor. There's no room to show visuals, so it's the power and focus of the words that have to connect. Go borrow an elevator and give your sound bites a try. You'll be ready when the pastor points to you and says, "Let's let our Volunteer Ministry Leader take 20 seconds to tell you about it."

> "A 'sound bite' is the sort of phrase that will stick with people . . . . Go borrow an elevator and give your sound bites a try. "

3. Who is your target audience?

There was a time when most volunteer recruiting messages were aimed squarely at stay-at-home moms. As noted earlier, that's a shrinking percentage of the population. These days you'd better think again about whom you want to reach with your marketing message.

This isn't a small thing. You must communicate your message in words that the audience understands, and highlight

Words to Avoid at All Costs

When crafting your marketing message, there are words you'll want to avoid. Good news: Here's a short list you can delete from your vocabulary before they get you in trouble! (Bad news: You'll probably discover other things to avoid as you work with volunteers.)

Worker. Who wants to be a "worker" in a ministry? The term denotes one of those bees who hauls pollen around all day so the Queen Bee can live in luxury. Call people volunteers, or staffers, or by their first names—but *don't* call them "workers."

Should. If this is your answer when people ask you why they might volunteer, you're dead in the water. Nothing turns off most people more than being told they *should* do something. That's a "push" word. Dig a little deeper and cast a "pull" vision that draws people *toward* the decision to volunteer.

Obviously. Okay, it's clear to you that people need to volunteer. But don't assume it's clear to them. They've not volunteered in the bell choir for 40 years and haven't run out of oxygen yet, thank you very much.

Duty. Ouch. This is a cousin to *should.* The clear implication is that failing to do what you've been asked to do is not just saying "no." It's *shirking* your duty.

Desperate. That you're desperate for a volunteer raises some questions you'd rather not raise: Why are you desperate? What do other people know that has convinced them to refuse? What aren't you telling me?

Anyone could do it. Do you mean it's so easy that it's meaningless, or that someone with the skills of a houseplant could accomplish the task? Either way, it's insulting.

What would Jesus do? Well, he might just ask you to wait until he was finished teaching to help you change the flat tire on the church bus. Or he might delegate the job to someone else. Jesus was a remarkable servant, but he *didn't* let himself be sidetracked from what was most important for him to accomplish in his ministry. Are you sure that your volunteer request is the most important thing the potential volunteer could be doing with his or her time?

benefits that the audience cares about. The language you select must connect with that audience.

Please note that you may have several campaigns running at the same time. You may be targeting:

Internal audiences—such as your pastor, board, or other governing body. Your message might be that there's a need for their support, endorsement, and involvement. You might also be building enthusiasm among the paid church staff for working with volunteers. You might be soliciting leadership's help in fundraising.

External audiences—as you recruit for additional volunteers, or a specific type of volunteer. You may be asking for time from people, or goods and materials from businesses. You might be asking young drivers to sign organ donor cards, or elderly people to donate used eyeglasses. You might want a volunteer to take over the Junior High youth group, or someone to help coordinate weddings scheduled at your church building.

Who's your audience? What do you know about those people? What do they care about? What's their situation in life—are they likelier to be married or single? Parents or not parents? Working, retired, or between jobs? Young or old? Do they have transportation or are they homebound? Are they leaders or followers? Are they conservative or liberal? Do they value stability and tradition or innovation and change?

And are there times they're so involved with other things that they simply won't pay attention to your message? For instance, if you're recruiting Sunday school teachers on Christmas morning, your timing is way, way off.

> "You want to speak their language."

The more you can identify the people you want to reach, the easier it is to reach them. You want to speak their language.

And don't think that this sort of market segmentation communication is something new. Consider what the Apostle Paul said about sharing the gospel:

Though I am free and belong to no man, I make myself a slave to everyone, to win as many as possible. To the Jews I became like a Jew, to win the Jews. To those under the law I became like one under the law (though I myself am not under the law), so as to win those under the law. To those not having the law I became like one not having the law (though I am not free from God's law but am under Christ's law), so as to win those not having the law. To the weak I became weak, to win the weak. I have become all things to all men so that by all possible means I might save some. I do all this for the sake of the gospel, that I may share in its blessings. (1 Corinthians 9:19-23)

Of course, you may be designing a marketing campaign that you want to reach everyone in your church. They're all over the map when it comes to age, health, and employment status. How can you target a message when there's no specific group of people to whom you want to aim your message?

Think again. There *are* commonalities in your church.

For starters, they all go to your church. They've accepted some common truths and beliefs. They probably all live in relatively close proximity. Many of them may know each other. They may agree on fundamental doctrinal issues. If you want to recruit five people to paint the Christian education classrooms, they've all seen the peeling paint. If you want to recruit ten people to do a community outreach program, they all know the neighborhood. If you want to recruit twenty people to feed and house members of a visiting choir, they all know their way back to church when it's time to deliver the choir members for a performance.

The nature of what you're trying to accomplish will help you find the common traits in potential volunteers, and help you select which volunteers to target.

Which leads to the next question . . .

4. What are your assumptions about your audience?

You aren't communicating in a vacuum. People in your audience already have feelings and beliefs about volunteering. They already have feelings and beliefs about themselves as volunteers, about you as a volunteer recruiter, about how volunteerism fits in your church, and about volunteerism itself.

Depending on how people feel and think, you may need to tailor your marketing message. For instance, if you're the sixth person this year who's tried to break through apathy and get someone—*anyone*—to volunteer, it's probably not a good idea to start with a pulpit announcement. Why? Because that's what all five of the other people did—and everyone in the audience has already said "no" five times.

> "People in your audience already have feelings and beliefs about volunteering."

You need to start somewhere else.

What can you discover or surmise about your audience? What do they know about the volunteer ministry? Is it positive or otherwise? Where did they get the information they have? How would they describe what a typical volunteer experience is like in your church?

Describe how you believe people feel and think about volunteering in your church. One description might be as follows:

> *Volunteering is for the old people in our church because they have lots of discretionary time. Once you sign up for a volunteer role, you're stuck in it until you die or Jesus comes back. Volunteers get honored once a year at a banquet, but that's about it—you never see them being thanked other than that. I should volunteer—I feel bad that I don't—but I'm a volunteer in other places like the Scouts and the kids' school. Except I don't think the pastor would count that as real volunteering because it's not at church.*

If those are thoughts running through your audience's mind, shouldn't your marketing message take these thoughts into consideration and address them?

It's not just the thoughts and feelings of the audience that impact your message; your thoughts, feelings, and assumptions play a part, too. Some of your assumptions might include . . .

- People are willing to give their time and resources if they're invested in a specific church program such as Sunday school, youth group, home visitation, or outreach.

- People expect to get something of value from their volunteer experience.

- People volunteer because they're asked directly.

- Volunteers are important people who have tremendous value.

- The church staff assumes that most volunteers aren't well trained or very reliable.

- The church staff thinks volunteers are nice to have, but aren't to be included in decision making.

- Some church staff thinks volunteers are more trouble than they're worth.

- Volunteers tend to quit unless their egos are stroked continuously.

What do you assume about volunteers? How do those assumptions aid or hinder your marketing message?

Four Tips for Creating an Effective Recruitment Message

1. Communicate a vision.

It's one thing to ask someone to be a worker in vacation Bible school. It's another to ask if someone would like to have the privilege of having an eternal impact for Christ in a child's life.

Communicating your need for volunteers won't motivate people; that's *your* problem. But inviting someone to join you in doing something important that will have an impact—*that's* worth doing.

2. Test your message.

What you easily understand may not be easily understood by others. Avoid slang, insider information, and abbreviations (for instance, not everyone knows that "VBS" stands for Vacation Bible School)—unless you use them strategically to connect with your target audience.

3. Communicate benefits without dwelling on them.

People want to feel noble when volunteering, not as if they're signing up just to get something in return.

4. Make it easy to respond.

How can someone get more information? Make it simple to follow up with a contact point. Provide a phone number, web site, brochure, physical information table—several options that provide the same simple, clear information. Make it easy to take the next step, and the more personal you can make the contact point, the better.

That said, sometimes there's value in making it *difficult* to respond.

At a local church, two sign-ups were under way after each worship service. One table was for the parish blood drive, and the recruiter was as close to the main door as possible so he could speak to everyone passing by. He had a sign-up sheet and schedule with him.

The woman recruiting teachers for an upcoming catechism class set her table up across the parking lot, inside the parish school, down the hallway in a classroom.

The blood donor recruiter told the woman, "You know, if you move your table over here by mine, you'll get a lot more people to sign up."

The woman smiled sweetly and said, "I'm not after people who need it to be convenient to sign up. I want people who are motivated enough to find me. You're after large numbers, so you're recruiting with a net. I'm after a very special sort of volunteer, so I'm fishing with a line."

What approach best suits your recruitment effort: a net or a line?

A rule of thumb: Spend more time on vision than logistics—it's the vision that will convince a potential volunteer that the role is both doable and worth doing.

5. What goals do you have for your marketing?

You need to define the outcomes of your marketing efforts if you hope to achieve them. And the more specific you are, the better you'll be able to determine if your plan got you where you wanted to go.

When you've finished your marketing efforts, what do you want people to know about your volunteer ministry? To say about it? What will your target audience be doing differently than what they're doing now? How many new volunteers will you have recruited or will you have reenlist? What evidence will point to the fact that your message was heard?

> "Be definite about your goals and write them clearly."

Keep in mind that if your marketing plan calls for you to bring people on board gradually, your plan should reflect that outcome in an appropriate timeline. It does you no good to recruit one hundred people today if you have nowhere for them to serve. If you expect to have one hundred positions gradually open throughout the coming year, write your marketing plan in such a way that it calls for you to recruit people at gradual intervals so nobody's time is wasted.

Be definite about your goals and write them clearly. If you don't aim at something specific, you won't know if you've accomplished what you set out to do—and that makes evaluating your efforts all but impossible.

When setting marketing goals—or any goals—include these elements:

- **Make marketing goals specific.**

"I want people in our church to know there are lots of ways they can volunteer" is too vague to be of any practical use. Force yourself to become more specific by determining *which* people you want to have knowledge . . . *what* they'll do to demonstrate they have knowledge . . . *where* they'll go as a result of having knowledge (to a volunteer orientation, hopefully!) . . . *when* they'll take action based on their knowledge

. . . and *why* they'll care about the knowledge they've gained.

Anything you can do to sharpen and focus a general marketing goal helps you accomplish it—because you know what you're aiming at.

A more specific way to phrase the goal presented above might be: "25 members of our church will attend a volunteer orientation program on February 10th, and 21 will be placed in volunteer roles by February 25."

- **Create marketing goals that are possible to attain.**

"Everyone in our church will be serving in a volunteer role this year" is a great goal. It's a *wonderful* goal. But is it likely you'll attain it?

Probably not.

There's nothing wrong with aiming high, but if you aim *too* high you'll just get discouraged. It's not necessarily a failure of your faith to set a goal that's more attainable. Should it be a challenge? Yes. Should it require faith? Certainly. But should it be realistic and attainable? Absolutely.

Goals must be achievements you're willing and able to work toward. If you set the bar high, that's motivational. If you set the bar so high there's no hope of your reaching it, that's unfair to you and anyone who's willing to help you.

> "Only you can determine if a goal is too high, too low, or just right."

If you have 45 people serving in volunteer roles this year, perhaps it would be a more realistic—yet challenging— goal to write, "As of April 10, 75 members of our church will be actively involved in volunteer roles."

Only you can determine if a goal is too high, too low, or just right. Do you believe that with God's help and hard work you just might reach it? Then it's probably a good goal.

- **Create marketing goals that have measurable outcomes.**

One measurement is time—set deadlines for the various steps in your marketing plan. If you intend to make an announcement from the pulpit on Sunday, which Sunday will it be? If you'll be personally contacting everyone in the church directory, when will you get to all the "A's?" All the "B's?" When will you finally be calling Zack Zuckerelli?

How many volunteers do you want to sign on? By when?

Marketing goals need observable results. You can count noses when it's time for a volunteer training event—so count noses. You can count the number of phone calls or personal visits you make, so count them.

One reason you make marketing goals measurable is to be able to track progress toward meeting them. Be sure to include time deadlines with each goal and sub-goal. The accountability is necessary.

Also, put a *name* next to each observable goal and sub-goal. Who is responsible for making it happen? If it's everybody, you're in trouble. Only when someone specific is accountable for achieving a goal will it actually happen.

> "Marketing goals need observable results."

As you move forward over time, it's likely you'll have to adjust your timing, tweak your budget, and reconsider which parts of your marketing plan require revision. Having observable goals lets you know where you are in the process.

A note: If you adjust your plan, keep track of those changes and update your written marketing plan. It's your master-planning document. Take time to document why and when you made adjustments—that information will help you do a better job of planning in future marketing cycles.

6. What are the benefits your volunteers can expect to receive?

Let's start by differentiating between features and benefits.

A feature is a *characteristic* of a product or service that's inherent in that service or product. For example, in a new car there are many features—power steering, air conditioning, and a gas gauge are among them.

A benefit is the *advantage* the user of the car receives because of the features. Power steering allows the driver to maneuver the car more easily. Air conditioning allows the driver to be comfortable in hot weather. And the gas gauge lets the driver avoid running out of gas and having to hike to the closest gas station!

What are the benefits your volunteers can anticipate receiving that you can include in your marketing message?

> "What are the benefits your volunteers can anticipate receiving?"

There was a time that few people would admit to volunteering for any reason other than pure altruism or discipleship. It was all about helping those less fortunate, and serving God.

Now the "What's in it for me?" question is raised more directly. It's not that people are no longer altruistic, but they're quicker to acknowledge that they have other motivations for volunteering as well. They're comfortable with the notion that it's okay to profit in some way from volunteer service.

This kind of profitability seldom comes in the form of money, though some volunteer service qualifies for tax breaks. Rather, volunteers also want to receive a nontangible benefit from their hours of service.

Not every volunteer role provides the same benefits. Not all benefits are equally desirable to each volunteer. But if you can present a variety of possible benefits for volunteers to consider, it may sweeten the deal when it comes to recruitment.

Among other benefits, these are some that may be available to volunteers:

Increased skills—If a teenager is planning to babysit for extra money, it never hurts to say that she's a regular volunteer in a church nursery.

Increased contacts—When someone volunteers, he or she makes contacts that can be leveraged for business or social opportunities. And in addition to those pragmatic concerns, friendships can quickly develop in a volunteer setting.

Volunteering is a way for those new to a church to be more quickly integrated into the faith community.

Increased knowledge—Someone who wishes to grow in a skill set may gain valuable experience in graphic design, sound engineering, or another area of expertise.

Increasing career potential—Networking that happens in a church volunteer setting can lead to new employment, or a reference that will enhance a resume.

Increasing self-awareness—By interacting with people in a volunteer setting, volunteers can expand their personal horizons and explore new situations and challenges. Volunteers often learn much about themselves.

Feeling accomplishment—Playing guitar in the worship band or serving in the church drama ministry might well satisfy a desire to perform that can't be met apart from joining the local community theater.

Satisfying a desire to give something back to the community or church—It's possible that someone who's volunteering at a homeless shelter today may have been a resident there just a few months ago. It's not uncommon for someone who's a tutor today to have benefited from a tutor's help in the past. There's a tremendous sense of satisfaction in helping another person.

Changing a volunteer's focus—If a volunteer is ill, depressed, lonely, or adjusting to loss in life, helping others can provide relief.

Raised self-esteem—Volunteers may feel better about themselves and their abilities because they're helping others. Also, they'll feel they are making a valuable contribution and may feel needed.

Recognition—A plaque or pin—something to hang on the wall of the study or wear on a lapel—may be the extrinsic reward that a volunteer craves.

What are the benefits that will be available to volunteers participating in your volunteer ministry? How have you made that information available?

Note that some volunteers consider it crass for you to

recruit on the strength of what's in it for the volunteers themselves. They want to think of themselves as primarily altruistic even as they consider which benefits might flow back to them. It's a wise volunteer manager who delivers the benefits that volunteers desire, but who treats those volunteers as if they're acting on the most noble motives possible.

7. How do you intend to deliver your marketing message to the target audience?

There are nearly endless possibilities for how to deliver your message.

You might attend scheduled church meetings and speak to people in groups such as worship services, committee meetings, and classes. Or you might send literature to people at home. You could call everyone directly. Then there's the face-to-face meeting, which is normally far more effective than any other technique at sharing your enthusiasm about the volunteer ministry—and recruiting additional volunteers.

Some factors that might influence which communication channels you select include . . .

The task for which you're recruiting volunteers. If your goal is to recruit enough people to move chairs out of the church sanctuary after the morning worship service this weekend, you won't need to provide much training—or seek a long-term commitment. In that case, an announcement and call for a show of hands will probably do the job, especially if the call for volunteers comes at the end of the worship service in question.

Do you need one eye surgeon willing to go on a medical mission trip, or twenty people willing to bake two dozen cookies for the next potluck? Generally speaking, the more complicated the task or rare the volunteer skill set, the more direct your communication will need to be.

The number of volunteers you need. If you're in a church of five thousand people and you need three volunteers for a fairly simple role, stopping into one adult class to recruit volunteers may accomplish the goal.

If you're seeking hundreds of volunteers, you'll need to

contact lots of people. A mailing is one option, but so is training a team of volunteer recruiters who will make personal contacts on your behalf.

Your budget. Your marketing plan will cost more than just time, though staff time and volunteer hours may be the most expensive item on your budget. Every activity will have a financial cost associated with it.

If you expect to do mailings, contact the post office or a mail center to determine the most cost-efficient way to make use of letters, brochures, or newsletters. If you intend to create teams to do marketing activities, then also figure in food and other reasonable costs.

Make the budget information available to people who are responsible for marketing activities, by the way. They need to know how much money—and time—they have to spend.

The time available. When you're planning the Christmas cantata and it's July, that's one thing. When the river's hit flood stage and Civil Defense needs people to haul sandbags, that's another situation altogether.

> "Your marketing plan will cost more than just time."

There are times a "phone tree" can be effective because the need for volunteers is immediate, and the cause so compelling very little explanation is needed.

Seek to plan far enough ahead when recruiting and using volunteers that you do *not* need to make use of instantaneous recruitment strategies. They may work once, but there's a diminishing return. Remember what happened to the proverbial boy who called "wolf" once too often: He lost the ear of his audience and suffered for it.

And when it comes to getting the most "bang for your buck," there's one way to reach your target audience that has far more impact than any other: word of mouth.

Word of Mouth Marketing

There's no more powerful way to market your volunteer ministry than through current volunteers. When a current volunteer tells friends that it's a great thing to sign up, that's a recruitment message that no number of slick brochures can equal.

Your current volunteers are your absolute best recruiters. They know the positions, they know your culture, and they know people like themselves.

Be intentional about word of mouth advertising. It may not occur to your current volunteers that they can recruit additional volunteers unless you encourage them to do so.

Here's how to create a successful Word of Mouth Marketing Campaign. It costs you nothing . . . but brings huge returns!

- **Create a super volunteer environment.**

Unless current volunteers love spending time in their roles, they'll never recommend a friend to do the same. Ask yourself: "Is what we do worthy of praise? Is how we do it worthy of praise? Are the results we're seeing worthy of praise?" If the answer to any of those questions is less than an enthusiastic "yes," you're not ready for a word of mouth marketing campaign.

Why? Because what is being said won't be positive.

When your process is praiseworthy (ask your volunteers to let you know when that happens), then it's time to go to the next step.

- **Find and thank champions.**

Not every volunteer will be willing to talk up your volunteer ministry. Identify those who will—and those who are effective at bringing in new referrals and volunteers. Go out of your way to thank them and encourage them to keep up the effort!

- **Bring your champions into the information loop.**

You don't want them giving misinformation—or old information. Be sure you brief them and provide every possible reason that they could recruit a new volunteer for you.

8. What marketing content do you want to deliver?

You have a purpose statement. You've written your sound bites. You've identified what matters to your target audience.

You know which benefits you can offer to your volunteers. You have an idea how you might want to connect with your target audience.

But all that makes very little difference if you have nothing to say.

Firm up the content you'll deliver in your marketing message. What is the central message you want to deliver?

When marketing your volunteer ministry, there are some things you simply *can't* say.

• Volunteering won't necessarily make participants rich— at least monetarily.

• Volunteering won't necessarily make participants younger—at least on the outside.

• Volunteering won't necessarily make participants more attractive to the opposite sex—but it certainly couldn't hurt!

The fact is that most of the benefit-promising marketing messages used to sell investments, skin cream, and baldness remedies just aren't available to you . . . but it's no real loss.

You *can* with integrity communicate that in volunteering there's deep fulfillment and meaning. That through volunteering a person can impact lives forever—and for the good. That through the touch of volunteers people who have no homes can find housing, people who seldom smile can find joy, and people who were once unable to read now can be employable.

> "In volunteering there's deep fulfillment and meaning."

You can craft a message that talks about significance, not sensuality. That's a message Coca-Cola® would love to own—but they don't. They never will. It's *your* message to share because the work you do connects people with people at a profound level.

Don't focus on what you can't say and promise. Focus on what *only* you can say.

As you craft your message, remain mindful of these points . . .

Keep your message simple.

No one wants to have to decipher your message. Be sure your audience never has to work hard to sort out what you're saying. And make responding to your message very, very easy.

For instance, rather than making volunteers figure out that to sign up they can call the church office and leave a message at 555-CARE, just list the phone number. Especially among older volunteers whose bifocal vision no longer appreciates small print, being forced to peck out the right buttons on a phone isn't appreciated.

Keeping your message simple sounds easy, but in fact it's very difficult to resist the temptation to complicate things. The benefit of simplicity is that it focuses on the quality and truth of your presentation, not on the gee-whiz theatrics of PowerPoint text swinging in from every possible direction on the screen.

> "Keeping your message simple sounds easy, but in fact it's very difficult."

Simplicity eliminates distractions and lets your audience focus on the central message.

Make sure your message reflects the tone of your volunteer ministry.

If it's fun to volunteer, say so. Show happy people interacting with other happy people in brochures and video clips. Talk about the friendships that have developed.

At one church in a northern state, the youth group got together after each heavy snowfall and shoveled the walks and driveways of elderly church members. The goal was to get to a home and shovel it—always at night, when the youth group members could meet—without being detected by the resident.

"Operation Snow" was a successful volunteer service project, but few in the youth group would have described it as such. To them it was the chance for buddies to pile into a station wagon and have fun while sneaking around at night. Friendships were the big draw; helping others by shoveling was a secondary outcome.

When recruiting for new volunteers, Operation Snow crew members talked about the sneaking—not the shoveling.

Be accurate in crafting your message.

While it's true that some volunteer positions save lives and make the world a better place, some volunteer positions fall a bit short of that. Folding bulletin covers is not quite as heroic as teaching the toddlers. Both roles are important; but don't portray the bulletin-folding job as on a par with taking the gospel to China. Never exaggerate, because people aren't fooled and you'll only diminish your credibility.

> "If it's fun to volunteer, say so."

Rather, describe the benefits of folding bulletin covers when you do it weekly with three friends around a table at the church building. It's a social time that includes fun, friendship, and donuts.

Grab the attention of your target audience.

That's easier said than done, but here are three tips for creating marketing messages that cut through the clutter of information overload and impact audiences.

• **Make the message personally relevant.**

If you're an 81-year-old widow, it's unlikely any marketing effort on behalf of the Young Marrieds Bible study group will motivate you to attend a meeting.

People tend to pay attention to things that have implications in their own lives, especially if what's being marketed appeals to their own personal goals, values, or felt needs.

One need felt by almost everyone everywhere is the need for more time. If you can honestly portray your volunteer ministry as making a huge impact in a limited amount of time, that's going to be well received. Don't ask people to "set aside a full week to support missions in Haiti by going to serve people."

Instead, ask them to "impact lives in a short-term, one-week missions trip."

See the difference? The first message sounds like a huge

investment. A *full week*? Who's got a *full week* to spare? The second message sounds like less of a time commitment, though both messages refer to the same seven days.

We also tend to pay attention when people portrayed in marketing efforts look like us, act like us, and seem to care about the things we care about.

Here's how you can put that tendency to use: On your volunteer web page and in your announcements use people who resemble the folks you're trying to reach. If you're after building attendance in your family night activities, show families. If you want leaders for the men's group rafting trip, show men who look like they could handle a raft.

- **Make the message enjoyable.**

People are drawn to things that make them feel good. That's one reason guilt is a poor marketing tool—it simply doesn't feel good. People avoid it.

You can make your marketing message enjoyable in several ways:

Excellent visuals. Don't settle for dark or muddy pictures, or static visuals. Take the time to capture images that are attractive, fun, and are of top-notch quality. It's worth the investment. And don't forget the power of showing your volunteers in action.

Engaging sound. If someone is doing a voice-over for a prerecorded announcement or recruitment video, use a voice that's easy to understand and sounds attractive. That's not to say you have to hire an expensive voice-over artist; using too "slick" a voice might actually backfire and alienate your audience. You don't need a voice professional—just someone who can speak with enthusiasm and clarity.

If you use music in your marketing, be sure the music you select is appropriate to your message and your audience. Music hooks emotions; be sensitive to what emotions you might be snagging. And respect copyrights when you select music—if it's illegal to use a song and you do so anyway, you signal to your audience that you aren't to be trusted. After all, you've just broken the law.

Easy readability. If you do a print piece, make it easy to read. Don't let a designer overpower your message with creative design. In the same way, use simple words in a straightforward fashion. Never make your audience work hard to decode what you're saying.

And a word about humor. Avoid it. It's dangerous, and a joke or cartoon in your brochure grows tiresome after a few readings. Can humor be used effectively and make a marketing message enjoyable? Absolutely. But realize that what's funny to one person isn't funny to the next person. Why take the risk?

- **Make the message unpredictable.**

It's predictable to *you*, of course, but it shouldn't be easily predicted by the person on the receiving end of the message.

If a message is novel, odd, or unexpected, it grabs attention because it's involving and new. Those two qualities require a great deal of creativity, of course, but the impact is worth the effort—*so long as the novelty doesn't obscure the message.*

Use this approach sparingly, and always test it before incorporating it widely in your marketing. It has great potential to confuse as well as amuse.

- **Use testimonials.**

In every brochure, video, PowerPoint presentation, and announcement about volunteer opportunities, include a testimonial. Why? Because people are skeptical when *you* tell them about a volunteer position. As the person recruiting volunteers, *you* need volunteers, right? So it stands to reason you'll say anything to recruit someone and solve your problem.

That means you have low credibility simply because it's perceived that you will benefit when someone raises a hand and volunteers.

But when someone *else* says that volunteering is rewarding—someone perceived to be objective—then the words carry more weight.

Is this fair? No. Is it necessarily accurate? Of course not—but it's real. Why do you think that companies selling weight loss programs always show you a happy customer who recommends the program?

Take this a step further. When it's time to make an announcement about volunteering, be sure it's a *volunteer* who makes the announcement.

Collect testimonials from your dedicated volunteers and keep them on file. Start now. You can use them when the opportunity presents itself, but not if you haven't got them in hand.

And here's a bonus: When a volunteer gives you permission to use his or her testimonial, it builds greater loyalty in the volunteer providing the glowing words.

Here are five tips for using testimonials effectively in your marketing:

> "Collect testimonials from your dedicated volunteers and keep them on file."

1. The time to ask for testimonials is toward the *beginning* of a volunteer's experience. There's a "honeymoon period" in most volunteers' involvement. That's the time when volunteers are likely to be most positive, and when the volunteer is most in touch with the benefits the experience is bringing to his or her life.

2. The more specific the testimonial, the better. It's one thing to say, "Serving in the nursery is good" and another to say, "Serving in the nursery let's me help families build a spiritual foundation in the precious children the families entrust to me."

3. Ask volunteers to make mention of your purpose or mission in their testimonial. If your ministry to special needs children is designed to build relationships as well as provide education, ask the volunteer to say so—if it's true in the volunteer's experience.

4. If the person giving the testimonial is credentialed in a relevant way, include the credentials. It's great

that a parent likes your Sunday school. It's especially great if a parent who's *also* a professional educator likes your Sunday school.

5. Always, always, *always* get permission to use testimonials. Never assume.

9. How will you evaluate your marketing efforts?

Your marketing efforts will grow stronger if you incorporate the classic feedback loop used by businesses when they track marketing impact: Action, Observation, Adjustment, Next Action.

Here's how it works . . .

Action describes the effort you make to market your volunteer ministry. For example, you launch a campaign to staff the choir with capable singers.

Observation describes your checking back to see if you were successful in meeting your marketing objectives. Are there enough sopranos in the first pew?

Adjustment describes the tweaking you'll do in light of the results of your marketing efforts. If you were able to recruit all the women singers you needed but you didn't land any men, you might want to redefine your target audience, or at least adjust the channels of communication you're using.

> "Some evaluation is built right into the system."

Next Action describes the new approach you're using. After giving it time to have an effect, you'll again observe the outcome . . . make adjustments . . . and act again.

Note that some evaluation is built right into the system because you identified desired marketing objectives that are observable and easily checked. (Good for you! Here's where the hard work is paying off!)

However, some other information will require digging.

Your budget, for instance—how are you doing? Are you under, on, or over? And how are you doing when measured against your timeline?

10. What trends and realities threaten your success?

When motion pictures transitioned from silent films to "talkies," even some top actors and actresses found their careers were suddenly over. Why? Because now that their voices could be heard, they lost their appeal.

Clara Bow, who had enjoyed a hugely successful career in silent films, fared less well on the silver screen when her thick Brooklyn accent was audible. Within a few short years, her film career was over. Technology had killed it.

Technology impacts your volunteer ministry, too—but how? Is it helping you or hindering you? How can you harness it to use it to your advantage? Consider not just the trends discussed at the beginning of this volume, but the following threats and opportunities listed below:

- **What trends in your community are working for or against volunteerism?**

If your local high schools require volunteer service for students in a civics class, how can you position your church so it is a recipient of volunteer hours? You wouldn't use part-time unchurched teenagers in your midweek program, but you can leverage the class requirement with your own teenagers to let them fulfill the requirement as they explore church ministries.

And perhaps the new swing set you want built in the play area could be constructed by unchurched kids?

The economy also has an impact as adults find they're either more—or less—available to volunteer hours for projects.

- **What organizations are competing with you for volunteer hours?**

Perhaps it seems uncharitable to think of other worthwhile organizations as competition, but you're all looking for volunteer involvement, and there's a limited pool of volunteer hours.

What organizations are your primary competitors? When you talk to people who tell you they're already involved in service, where are they volunteering? You may discover that the local hospital auxiliary or library board is staffed with people you'd love to have leading small groups in your church.

The questions you need answered are these: Why is volunteering for your competition so attractive? What are the benefits received by those volunteers? What can you learn from other organizations about how to structure your volunteer ministry?

- **Are changes happening in your community or church?**

Things change—and your marketing message may need to change with them to match a shifting demographic or environment.

Has your church had a large influx of older people? younger people? homeschoolers? people who are wealthier or less wealthy than your existing membership? Is your leadership shifting direction regarding worship style, number of services, or approach to Christian education? Change isn't a bad thing, but it can certainly impact your volunteer ministry.

> "Things change—and your marketing message may need to change with them."

The pastor of a church in the West came up with a great solution to fix the problem of an overcrowded sanctuary: Go to two services. The parking lot congestion would be lessened, the congregation wouldn't be sardined into the pews—it seemed like a "no-brainer" when he suggested it to the church board. The pastor wanted to make the change in 30 days.

Fortunately, several board members happened to be people who have volunteer recruitment functions in the church. Both the children's church and Sunday school superintendents pressed the pastor for details: What would happen to their programs?

The pastor thought for a moment and then shrugged. "You'll do two Sunday schools and two children's church programs, I guess."

The church did make the change—not in 30 days, but eventually—and the superintendents did double their volunteer staffs to accommodate the change. But had the change been made in just a few weeks, as the pastor proposed, it would have been chaos.

Stay abreast of changes that will impact your volunteer ministry. For community information, talk with local business reporters and local chambers of commerce. Real estate agents often see trends develop early on as well.

To stay in touch with changes in your church, become an active participant on decision-making boards. Volunteer to serve there and you'll be amazed how quickly you get in the information loop!

A Brief Summary

Creating a marketing plan is the best way to be assured that your marketing efforts will be coordinated, focused, and consistent. And to create that plan you need to answer these ten questions:

1. What's the *purpose* of your volunteer ministry?

2. What can you *say*—in a "sound bite"—about your volunteer ministry?

3. Who is your *target audience*?

4. What are your *assumptions* about your audience?

5. What *goals* do you have for your marketing?

6. What are the *benefits* your volunteers can anticipate receiving?

7. How do you intend to *deliver* your marketing message to the target audience?

8. What marketing *content* do you want to deliver?

9. How will you *evaluate* your marketing efforts?

10. What *trends and realities* threaten your success?

Don't rush the process of answering these questions. Any time you invest in creating a marketing plan will be returned many times over as you avoid off-target campaigns, last-minute decisions, and wasted efforts.

Keep your written marketing plan where you can refer to it often. It's your blueprint for marketing success. You'll want it handy.

Though there's no particular format a marketing plan should follow, we've provided some worksheets on pages 98-103. Use them to help you walk through the process described above.

Communicating about your volunteer ministry clearly and regularly is a key to successfully involving people in ministry opportunities. But *which* ministry opportunities? There may be no shortage of people in your church willing to help out with the Easter Festival, but when the Missions Fair rolls around, there's a distinct echo in the room when you ask for volunteers. Nobody responds. You're talking to yourself.

> **"Are people in the right jobs?"**

And why is it that your volunteers in one area of ministry seem to stick forever, effectively serving others and glorifying God, when you can't keep a Sunday school teacher for more than six months?

The answers to those questions can become complex, but there's an obvious place to start: Are people in the right jobs? If they aren't, you can count on frequent turnover, burned out volunteers, and a distinct lack of enthusiasm for volunteerism in your church. When a square peg is pounded into a round hole, it's no fun for either the peg *or* the hole.

The solution: Place the right people in the right jobs.

And you can accomplish that with interviews.

THREE
Interviewing Prospective Volunteers

How to get yourself and your church ready. Building a team of interviewers. The four-step interview process explained.

The context in which most of us have encountered interviews is when we've tried to land a job. And with few exceptions, the interviews have been nerve-wracking experiences.

We spend the days leading into the interview composing answers to the questions we most expect to hear from the Personnel Manager who's sitting behind a desk, pencil in hand as she fires off one question after another.

My biggest weakness? *That's probably my tendency toward being a work-a-holic* (a trait we secretly hope will be viewed as a virtue by a potential employer), *and maybe my near-obsession for excellence.*

The reason I left my last position? *It was a mutual decision, based on the changing demands of the marketplace* (I'd have had to learn to actually touch-type, but I won't mention *that*).

> "Interviews tend to be carefully choreographed experiences."

Interviews tend to be carefully choreographed experiences, with the person being interviewed determined to reveal only what's most positive and likely to impress the interviewer. For the person being interviewed, it's a sales presentation with the sole goal of getting a job offer.

Meanwhile, the person doing the interviewing is attempting

to kick over rocks and see what's hidden beneath. Does the interviewee have the skills needed to be successful? Will he fit into the corporate culture? Is there something lurking just beneath the surface that would be helpful to know—but is being concealed?

What's missing in many interviews is a desire to understand and be understood—to lay cards on the table and see if there's a good combination.

No wonder that when many churches hear that interviews are essential for a well-run volunteer ministry, eyebrows shoot up. After all, if people want to volunteer, why not just let them? They already know what they want to do, right?

Not necessarily.

Let's take a look at what volunteer interviews are—and what they aren't.

The Volunteer Interview

Volunteer interviews aren't an experience in which the involved parties are trying to avoid being honest and open. Just the opposite—they're helpful *only* if everyone at the table is seeking the same goal: *to put the right person in the right job.*

Here's the rub: Potential volunteers—people who've decided to commit time and energy to serving in and through your church—often don't know what's really involved in each volunteer role. And they usually don't know the complete range of volunteer roles available to them.

Consider: On a typical Sunday morning a typical church member—let's call him Bob—may see only a few roles being filled by volunteers. The greeter, usher, and people who take up the offering are probably all volunteers, as is Bob's Sunday school teacher. And it's probable the people in the worship band are volunteers, too, but that's about it. If Bob doesn't see himself in any of those specific roles, he may decide there's nowhere he fits as a volunteer.

What Bob *doesn't* see is the administrative assistant in the church office on Monday morning. The altar care coordinator who organizes a team that keeps the front of the sanctuary visually interesting. He never sees all the boards meet to do the business of the church, and the follow-up and visitation teams aren't on Bob's radar. The people who write and prepare the bulletins and newsletters aren't obvious, nor are the six guys who keep the building and grounds in tip-top shape.

The youth sponsors are serving elsewhere in the building, as are most of the children's ministry leaders. And someone's going to count the money in the offering plates and handle church finances on Sunday afternoon—though Bob won't see that happen.

Bob isn't even aware that the church has periodic short-term mission trips, or that the big room downstairs with all the groceries in it is a food pantry for the community.

> "Potential volunteers . . . usually don't know the complete range of volunteer roles available to them."

Had Bob turned around to look, he'd have seen Susan running the sound board and John recording the pastor's sermon for distribution to shut-ins, who will be visited on Monday evening. Dale and Patty deliver those tapes and a healthy dose of encouragement every week.

There are search and personnel committees, small group ministries, singles ministries, and college ministries Bob knows nothing about—and they're all run by volunteers. A prayer team is praying for the morning worship experience even as Bob sits in church, but he doesn't know it.

The wedding Bob will attend next Saturday at the church will be coordinated by a volunteer, but Bob won't be aware of the hours Nancy has put into making sure everything is just right for the bride—and the bride's mother.

Bob has placed himself on the sidelines as a volunteer not because he's apathetic, but because he has no vision for the scope of your church's volunteer ministries.

You think Bob's a slacker. After all, he's an elementary teacher who refuses to teach Sunday school, although he's a natural. After asking him twice to take over the second-grade class and being turned down flat, you're wondering about Bob's salvation. How can a Christian be so callous about serving God?

Here's what you don't know about Bob: He's tired of teaching. After 23 years in the classroom the last thing he wants to do is spend weekends doing the same thing he does all week long.

But he *is* an avid photographer. He often wonders why the church doesn't do more with the projection unit that's hanging from the ceiling, but he's never thought to ask. And he's just gotten a grant from the State to develop a training program for the teachers in the district. Bob's a Master Teacher who actually enjoys helping teachers fresh out of college master the real-world skills they need to deal with challenging kids.

You don't know Bob—and he doesn't know the volunteer opportunities in his own church. Not the ones that would excite him and give him the chance to pursue his passions.

So Bob sits. Week after week. And your corporate worship experience isn't blessed with visually dynamic photographs to accompany the singing. Your struggling Sunday school teachers don't receive a seminar that would build their skills and increase their effectiveness.

How many Bobs are there in your church?

Would you like to get them involved?

The interview process is one way to do it. At an interview Bob would be able to express what he's passionate about—photography, training, and whatever else God has wired him to get jazzed about—and to hear the range of places he could put that passion to use. He'd get connected.

> "Volunteer interviews help put the right people in the right jobs."

That's what volunteer interviews do—connect people with volunteer roles. They help put the right people in the right jobs—to the benefit of the volunteers, for the good of the church, and to glorify God.

Volunteer interviews *are* about placing volunteers in the

right spots. Volunteer interviews *aren't* about judging people in an effort to eliminate them from service opportunities.

Volunteer interviews are also a wonderful place to do ministry. At church we spend much of our time listening. We hear sermons, teaching, and music. Plenty of information gets beamed our way. But how often do we get to be *heard*?

In the setting of a one-on-one interview with potential volunteers, you have the privilege of entering into the lives of brothers and sisters in Christ. You get to ask questions that get at what matters most to people, and then hearing what they have to say. The potential volunteers get valued and *heard*— and that's ministry.

How to Get Started with Volunteer Interviews

Before you dive into doing interviews, there are some things you need to do. Building an effective volunteer ministry is a process, and you'll sabotage your efforts if you do things out of order.

For the interview process to be effective, you need to be ready in two ways . . .

You need to be ready personally.

A question to consider: Do you *really* believe that everyone has something to offer in ministry? Truly, down deep, cross-your-heart-and-hope-to-die believe that God has gifted everyone with a skill, passion, talent, or ability that can be used to bless others and glorify God?

Because if you have any doubts about that, it's going to show in your ability to interview potential volunteers.

If you haven't reviewed carefully the Scripture passages outlined in volume 1 of this Volunteer Leadership Series, do so now. Ask God to impress on your heart *his* heart for letting very imperfect people do ministry in his name. It's one of the ways God shows us grace: He lets us do significant things that have eternal consequences.

Not one of the people you interview as potential volunteers will be perfect. Their skills won't be perfect. Their experience won't be perfect. Their thinking and demeanor won't be perfect. And that's as it should be—because *we aren't perfect people.*

So adjust your expectations and proceed accordingly. You're going to have to see people as God sees them, and place them accordingly. You (and/or your team of volunteer interviewers) must understand the goal of the process: *to get the right people into the right jobs.*

It's that simple.

You won't be attempting to sell anyone on a particular job that desperately needs to be filled. God already knows that position is open and he has someone in mind for it—but not necessarily the person you're interviewing. It's far, far better to leave a volunteer job empty than to fill it with the wrong person.

> "You're going to have to see people as God sees them."

You won't be offering career counseling or spiritually admonishing people to "name and claim" abilities, skills, or passions they don't currently have. God may choose to develop new attributes in people, but that's between them and God.

You *will* be carefully, prayerfully attempting to discover the uniqueness in each person you interview. You'll be presenting a variety of volunteer positions that might be of interest to the person you're interviewing. You'll seek to be clear, nonjudgmental, and reassuring.

Your goal is to get the right people into the right jobs. Are you ready to put that goal first in your interactions with potential volunteers?

Your church needs to be ready.

If 25 people raised their hands today and volunteered to show up next Sunday morning to help, where would you use them? Are you ready to give them the information they need to be effective? What would you do with a flood of volunteers?

A flood is exactly what might happen if you proactively interview people in your church and unleash the volunteer potential that's simmering out there in the pews.

We've long sighed and lamented how the old "80/20 rule"

seems to be the eleventh commandment in the church. We congratulate the 20 percent of the people who do 80 percent of the work, then wonder what could ignite a fire under the other 80 percent of the people who just show up and sit there.

Well, there's no sense getting people recruited if you're not ready to follow up. That will frustrate everyone.

Here are eight ways you'll want your church to be ready before you begin interviewing volunteers:

1. Your church leaders must be ready to share responsibility and power.

Not every church truly wants volunteers in significant positions. Sometimes it's fine if "new people" set up chairs and tables for the church social hour, but to make a suggestion about how to revitalize that event you have to have been born into the church. The advice of "newbies" isn't welcome.

If you've asked leaders of ministry areas to tell you what volunteer positions they want filled, and each position you've received is an entry level slot, that tells you something: Apparently there's not a willingness to share power. Or there's a deeply held belief that volunteers can do tasks, but not supervise people.

Those are not good signs that your church will be a culture where volunteers can grow in their skills and abilities. Before you continue with implementing volunteer interviews, meet with church leadership and explore any issues that might be fueling their concern about giving volunteers power and authority.

2. You have job descriptions in hand.

Until you have completed job descriptions—preferably written by the leaders who will supervise the volunteer roles described—you're not ready to interview volunteers. Why? Because you aren't ready to put the right people in the right jobs. You don't truly know what's involved in the jobs. You can't answer volunteers' questions.

And you aren't absolutely sure you have the buy-in from the leaders in every ministry area. A hesitation to fill out job descriptions can be one indicator of a lack of enthusiasm for the volunteer placement process.

Job descriptions are vitally important. A sample job description is on page 104. Use it as a template to teach your leaders how to create job descriptions for existing and proposed volunteer positions.

3. You have a team of volunteer interviewers.

Depending on how many interviews you need to conduct, a team approach to the task is essential. For the role of volunteer interviewer, it may actually be best *not* to ask for volunteers to fill the role. It's such a specific role that you may do better to handpick people to do the task.

When Marlene Wilson wanted to build a team of volunteer interviewers in her church, she sat down with her pastor and they looked through a church directory.

"We checked the ten to twelve people we individually felt would be the best candidates," says Marlene. After determining who had the skills to be effective, the candidates were contacted individually and asked to consider taking on the role. Each candidate agreed.

May you have a similarly happy result!

Here are the qualities Marlene Wilson suggests you look for in appropriate candidates . . .

Someone who is a genuinely friendly and approachable person.

The ideal candidate is likely someone who has a broad network of friendships and acquaintanceships already. They're engaging and warm.

Someone who cares about people.

Your top candidates may be serving in people-helping roles already, or working in the social sciences. The value of caring about people can be expressed in many ways, but it should be in evidence.

Someone who is a good listener.

Test this for yourself. Engage a potential candidate in

conversation, and pay attention to how the individual communicates empathy, warmth, and respect. Does it *feel* as if the person is listening? Do you hear follow-up questions that signal comprehension? Does it *look* like the person is listening? Is the candidate focused and attentive? Leaning forward and making eye contact?

Listening skills can be taught (and should be!), but you may not have time to do so before the interviews begin. Look for candidates who have a high degree of competence in this area already.

> *Someone who is trustworthy and with whom people will feel comfortable sharing personal information.*

This is really a two-fold requirement. The person must in fact be able to be trusted with information. Someone who is a gossip won't make a good volunteer interviewer. And the person must be *perceived* as trustworthy by others. Otherwise interviews won't reveal much because interviewees won't be open. See page 104 for a sample job description for this role.

4. You've decided whom to interview.

Churches approach this issue in a variety of ways.

Some churches begin with a church-wide interview, connecting with every member. That's the ideal, but depending on the size of your congregation it may be impractical.

Other churches interview people who pass through the new members class, and build a base of information that way. Still other churches begin the process with current leaders and those who aspire to leadership positions.

Mindful that your goal is to identify the abilities, skills, and passions that are available to do ministry in your church, and that you want everyone to have the opportunity to be effectively involved in ministry, the more people you interview the better.

Start small if necessary, but look forward to including as many people as possible. And don't forget that you are interviewing *all* the membership—*including* youth and children.

Young people have been given God-given abilities, skills, and passions, too. Don't forget to help them find significant, meaningful ministry opportunities.

5. You're ready to collect and safeguard information.

As you do interviews you'll be collecting personal information. Generally speaking, you need to treat it as confidential personnel information.

Before you begin interviewing, know where hard copies of the interview sheets can be kept in a secure environment. Know who will have access to the information—electronically or in hard copy. It may seem like a minor detail, but where *will* you put hundreds (or thousands) of pieces of information so they're secure and still available to the right people?

Decide now on what information storage and retrieval system you will use, *before* you collect information. If you're the person functioning as the Director of Volunteer Ministries— at least in part of your church's programming—let this be your responsibility. You'll reap the benefits if you see that it's done well.

If possible, use computer software to record and retrieve information. It requires keying in data, but once you've captured it, you've got it forever. Updating addresses and phone numbers is simple, as is sorting information.

You may already have a software program designed to track pledges, contributions, attendance, and other administrative functions. See if that program can be adapted. If not, conduct a quick web search for programs—there are dozens of them, always being updated. Visit Group's Church Volunteer Central at www.churchvolunteercentral.org for reviews of possible software selections.

Remember to set up different security levels so more than one user can utilize the software, and only appropriate people can get at sensitive data.

Sound too expensive? If you buy a software program and don't use it, it's very expensive. *Buy only what you'll use . . . and then use it.* Nothing is more expensive that a needless technology purchase.

If you want an inexpensive, down-and-dirty approach and you don't intend to ask for sensitive information, ask a computer savvy volunteer to set up a simple database in Microsoft Access or another database software. Even Excel spreadsheets are sufficient for small churches.

> "Buy only what you'll use . . . and then use it."

Some questions for you to consider before purchasing software:

- Does the proposed software meet our present needs, exceed our needs, or greatly exceed our needs?

- Can the software meet our needs if the size of our church doubles?

- Is it easy to use?

- Who'll use the software? What do those people think of the choice?

- Is training provided? By whom? When? How often?

- What kind of on-going support does the vendor provide? At what cost?

- Can multiple users access the software at varying security levels? How?

- Is our current computer hardware adequate to use the software? What upgrades might be required? Are we willing to make them? At what cost?

- Does purchasing this software contribute to our ability to fulfill our mission and meet our goals? In what ways?

6. You're ready to respond when unexpected information is revealed.

It may not happen often, but it will happen: You or one of your team of volunteer interviewers will discover uncomfortable information about a church member.

Generally, you aren't required to divulge what you discover to a local law enforcement agency unless you discover the individual is being hurt, is hurting or plans to hurt someone else, or is doing something illegal. Those are broad guidelines, though.

Determine what your approach will be before you begin interviewing people. What is your church policy? The policy recommended by your insurance carrier? What does the law require in your area? Do the homework now, mindful that interviews conducted with potential volunteers are an official function of your church's program.

Not every piece of unexpected information will necessarily trigger a call to law enforcement or social service authorities. But sometimes it *should* trigger a referral to a capable, qualified people-helper like a pastor or counselor.

> "Determine what your approach will be before you begin interviewing."

It was during an interview with a potential children's worker that one interviewer, Kim, asked the question, "What is it about this church that attracted you?"

The woman being interviewed became quiet and stared at her hands as a long moment passed. "At least here the pastor hasn't made a pass at me yet," she said finally, in a still, small voice. Then, eyes on fire, she leaned toward Kim and hissed, "That's what happened in my last church. I hope he rots in hell."

"It was like she turned into a different person," Kim remembers. "She took a couple of long breaths, shook her head, then with a smile, looked back up at me said, 'Well, then, any more questions?'"

Oh, yeah. Kim had a *lot* more questions—but none she was qualified to ask and process with the potential volunteer.

They finished the interview, then Kim suggested that before the woman enter into ministry at the new church she consider addressing the issues that she had with her experience at the last church.

"I told her that we'd walk through the process with her

every step of the way, and I looked forward to offering her a choice of volunteer positions. But she couldn't serve joyfully out of an abundant life when she wasn't experiencing one."

The woman heeded Kim's counsel and accepted a referral to the church's counseling ministry. A year later she was on board as a volunteer.

"She's doing great," Kim says, "But she wouldn't have been if we hadn't interviewed her and given her some direction. She'd just have *appeared* to be doing great."

What would you do in a similar situation? How would you refer her? Decide now so that you are ready.

7. Your church is ready to provide background screenings for potential volunteers.

The days when screening volunteers was the ultimate "extra mile" effort of ultra-careful churches are over. It's now something that needs to be part of your standard procedure. It protects your church, the volunteers who serve through your church, and most importantly, it protects children and youth.

Three decisions you need to make:

• What level of screening do you need?

In this world of computers you can arrange to have someone screened for practically anything. And not every volunteer position needs the same sort of background screening.

For instance, if Jerri is going to be handling the church checkbook, you'll want to know that her credit history and her use of money have been screened. Has she proven to be a capable steward in the past?

If Dave wants to work with a small group of children on Wednesday night, his use of credit is probably less important than whether he's been convicted of a crime, and if so, which crime.

You can arrange for background screenings in each of the following areas, and more:

Identification—Is the person operating under an alias?

Criminal records—Has the person been convicted of a crime?

Credit checks—Is the volunteer on a solid financial footing? This can be a general indicator of responsibility and financial skills.

Education and employment verification—Has the person lied about credentials or previous employment?

Department of Motor Vehicles—Is the person to be trusted transporting children or teenagers on trips?

Bankruptcies, liens, and judgments—Is the person in financial straits?

Civil lawsuits—Has the person been a plaintiff and/or a defendant, and if so, how many times? Is the person prone to settling conflict through litigation?

Screening—at a price—can also uncover real estate holdings, marital history, residences, and bank assets. Almost anything that someone wants to hide can be dragged into the light.

And the screenings can be conducted just for your local area, your state (or province), your country, or internationally. It's all available—at a cost.

You want to strike a balance that makes background searches affordable and effective. It's doubtful that Bill, who you've known for years and who grew up in the church, has shady international business dealings in Dubai.

Contact your insurance provider and ask for guidelines. That will let you know what level of screening is generally recommended, and may also qualify you for a rate discount because you've put the procedure in place. Contact other churches in your area, too. What sort of screening do they require? Why did they settle on that level?

What happens if you find that someone has been convicted of a crime? What crimes will disqualify someone from volunteering in a specific area, and which crimes aren't a problem? After all, getting three speeding tickets in a year is one thing if Larry wants to volunteer in the bulletin stuffing ministry, and quite another if he wants to drive the church bus.

And get in touch with several screening providers. If you're a member of Group's Church Volunteer Central, you can get screenings at a variety of levels at a significant discount. Take advantage of this opportunity—the savings on screenings alone can more than pay for your membership each year.

• **Who will you screen?**

Not every volunteer role involves the same risks. Generally speaking, if a volunteer has contact with children or youth, that volunteer needs to be screened. Discuss other guidelines with your insurance carrier, other churches, and the screening provider you hire. And again, if you're a member of Group's Church Volunteer Central, ask for guidelines from that organization, too.

You'll need to decide what to do if a potential volunteer is new to your area. Will you screen both locally and in that person's previous place of residence? What if, after several years of service, a volunteer switches from a role where there's been no contact with children to the role of fourth-grade Sunday school teacher?

It's critical that you put policy decisions in place before you begin interviewing volunteers, and that once those policies are in place you *never make an exception*. Perhaps Mrs. Wazniak *has* been teaching children's church for 35 years. That's wonderful—give her a certificate of appreciation . . . and a screening.

• **How will you advertise that you screen volunteers—and when?**

Screening is a safety net—your last chance to keep someone who has already lied to you twice (you asked about convictions on your application and in the interview, right?) from having access to the people you serve, and to your other volunteers.

People who have been convicted of a crime tend to fear screenings. They know if they're listed in a sexual offender database that their names will pop up. They know if they've been imprisoned or involved in the court system that it's going to come out. So if they know you're going to screen them, they tend to not even attempt to volunteer.

So announce that you'll be screening at the interview stage

of your recruitment and placement process. Why? So people have a chance to tell you about their issues, rather than hiding them from you.

If a potential volunteer says, "Look—I can tell you right now that if you screen my records you'll find out I spent a year in jail for car theft when I was 19 years old. That was 23 years ago and I've long ago repented. I've not taken so much as a stick of gum that wasn't mine since, and I never will. God has changed my life."

That's a very different situation than someone who chooses to remain silent, waiting to see if your screening turns up a past conviction.

> "Let potential volunteers know early on that screening is mandatory."

Let potential volunteers know early on that screening is mandatory if you intend to screen them. You'll need their approval, and if someone refuses, you may have kept a wolf out of the sheep pen.

What's your plan for screening potential volunteers? Is it in place? And have you and your team already gone through the process?

It may be that to do what you're doing you don't need to be screened. It would save your church money if you weren't screened. You've never been arrested or convicted of a crime and you know for a fact you'll come up clean when you're screened.

Do it anyway, and here's why: You'll be able to tell anyone who is offended by being asked to go through a police screening that you've been through the same procedure. That fact will stop a lot of arguments before they start.

Yet, you may find that if you *start* screening volunteers, you offend the faithful volunteers who have served for years. How can you navigate that quagmire?

- Explain that everyone will be screened—and include *everyone.*

- Explain that results are confidential, and detail how information will be safeguarded.

- Be clear on what levels of screening you're including for various volunteer positions. This will reduce fear among people who have had ancient run-ins with the law, or who fear embarrassment about past decisions.

- Talk about the church's need to be viewed as a safe place by visitors who don't know the character of long-term volunteers. It's not a personal thing; it's a sign-of-the-times thing.

- Stand firm. Seek to understand a volunteer's concerns, but if the decision is that everyone will be screened, everyone will be screened.

- Determine how you'll go about responding if someone is found to have a criminal background. Will you separate volunteers from service? Will you keep volunteers in place if they've demonstrated healing and repentance? Will you offer volunteers who are screened out of one position the chance to serve elsewhere?

8. You're ready to make a handoff to the appropriate volunteer leader.

Once a potential volunteer is interviewed, where will you send the person? In each area of ministry where a volunteer will be used there must be someone designated to do the follow-up interview. As you'll see in the next section, *you* won't actually offer anyone a volunteer position. You'll simply refer a volunteer to an area where you think they'll flourish. It's up to someone in that area to determine if the volunteer and a volunteer role are a fit.

If in your best judgment you think someone would make a great youth volunteer, is the Youth Ministry Director ready to follow up? If not, don't send anyone to the youth department until that leader *is* ready.

Being "ready" comes down to this: Are resources in place for training and orientation that will make the volunteer successful? Have you removed as many institutional and personal obstacles to volunteering as possible? Do you have a compelling vision for what God will do through and in you as volunteers grow involved in new ways?

Is your marketing message tight and focused? Your strategy for marketing set? Your planning finished?

Yes? Then contact the people whom you think will make good interviewers, get them on board, and begin training them.

How to Train Your Interview Team

First, a principle to embrace: The more your interviewers do at the front end of your interview and placement process, the less you will have to fix later.

It's true. Interviewers are key players in the process. They have an enormous influence on whether potential volunteers eventually become practicing volunteers. You want your team of interviewers to be as effective as possible.

And to be effective, your team must have both information and skills. The data you can pass along in printed form, and it's probably best to do so in a three-ring binder. Why? Because you'll be updating it frequently. Whether you have a team of one or one hundred, decide how you'll go about getting updates into the hands of your team and formalize that process.

Here's what your team must know . . .

Interviewers must know about your church.

Give your interviewers a copy of your church's mission statement and vision statement. Provide copies of your volunteer ministry's mission and purpose statements, too. Discuss them thoroughly, and how the interviewers will be cooperating in helping bring those missions and purposes to life.

Be sure your interviewers know about the major ministry areas and initiatives in your church and how those ministries wish to be described. Your interviewers are gateways for volunteers entering church ministries; if their information is spotty or incomplete, it will show in the quality of referrals made.

If at all practical, have the leaders in those ministry areas meet your interviewers. As a potential volunteer is interviewed and then referred for a follow-up interview and placement, you want the process to be as seamless as possible. It all works best when there's at least some relationship between the people in the process.

Consider creating a notebook of information for your volunteers, and make sure information is consistent across every volunteer's notebook. While different interviewers will have different styles, the experience should be equally informative.

Interviewers must know relevant policies and procedures.

Where do surveys go when they're completed? What tools are available for introducing potential volunteers to possible job matches? What's the timeline from the completion of the first interview to the next step? What *is* the next step? How do you make a referral? Those are the sorts of practical questions your interviewers will have—and they'll need answers.

You'll enhance interviewers' comfort level if you anticipate at least some of the questions they'll have and proactively provide information. Then ask what other questions they have and provide that, too. One church leader has this philosophy: "Any time I hear the same question twice, I create a policy and print a brochure."

You may not want to go to the trouble of creating a brochure, but the information should certainly go onto an updated "Frequent Questions" sheet in your interviewers' notebooks.

Interviewers must have skills, and among these are three skills that are essential for a successful interview. Here's what your team must be able to do . . .

1. Interviewers must be able to put people at ease.

Part of this skill is to conduct interviews in a setting that's free of interruptions and that's physically comfortable. It may be a room or office at your church, but it can just as easily be a coffee shop where you can sit in a quiet corner booth. The chief requirement is that you find a place you can talk for 30 or 40 minutes without the flow of the conversation being broken, and without being overheard.

If you *do* use an office, avoid having a desk separate the interviewer and potential volunteer. Set the phone so it won't ring. Communicate in every way throughout the duration of the interview that nothing is more important than the person being interviewed.

But even if the lighting is fine, the temperature perfect, and the chairs comfy, people being interviewed may still feel ill at ease.

What *really* relaxes people is how interviewers conduct themselves. Is the interviewer rushed, or relaxed? Is the interviewer open and respectful? Is the interviewer able to converse easily and listen carefully? Does the person being interviewed feel important and heard, or perceive that the interviewer is just plodding through paperwork?

> "What *really* relaxes people is how interviewers conduct themselves."

Remember: The interview is an opportunity for the interviewer to minister to the potential volunteer. Your interviewers must be primarily people-focused, not task-oriented, as they conduct interviews. As they master the interview process they may in fact choose to not even take notes unless it's absolutely necessary. Note-taking breaks eye contact and may make the potential volunteer uneasy. It's best if interviewers can remember what was said well enough to fill in the paperwork immediately after the interview ends.

Also, coach interviewers to speak clearly and explain things patiently, preferably without using coded language. It's easy in a church setting to assume that everyone knows when "Advent" is, or what "Communion preparation" means. A potential volunteer may nod politely as if understanding but in fact be totally in the dark. It's better to over-explain than assume comprehension.

2. Interviewers must be able to ask appropriate and meaningful questions.

This takes practice to interview with grace, so plan to train your interviewers even if they have strong people skills. In fact, *especially* if they have strong people skills.

Sometimes interviewers who love spending time with people tend to fill the first half of any interview time with chit-chat, sharing stories from their own lives. Establishing rapport is fine, but it can't take over an interview session. Nor can selling the potential volunteer on the wisdom of signing up to volunteer, or reviewing facts that aren't really relevant until a potential volunteer is offered a position.

Some interview skills to sharpen in your volunteer team . . .

- *Ask open-ended questions and make open-ended statements.*

An open-ended question or statement is one that can't be answered with a simple "yes" or "no" and usually reveals far more information than a directive, closed-ended question.

For instance, a closed-ended, directive question might be, "Do you have a family?" You'll get an answer, but it might very well be just "yes" or "no." Instead, ask for family information in the form of an open-ended question or statement such as, "Tell me about your family." The answer will likely be something along the lines of "Yes, a husband and two children," followed by details.

One simple way to train your volunteers to use open-ended questions naturally is to have them form trios and practice on each other by assigning three roles: Interviewer, Interviewee, and Observer. Select a subject such as "My Last Vacation" and have the members of each trio take turns in the different roles.

Using open-ended questions is a habit your interviewers must form. And it *is* a habit—practice is essential.

- *Ask linking questions.*

A linking question is one that ties to something the person being interviewed has just said. It's an invitation to go deeper, to explain and explore more fully. A linking question communicates that the interviewer is actively listening, not just running down a list of questions and gathering the least amount of data needed.

Here's an example of linking questions following an open-ended statement:

Interviewer: Tell me about your favorite volunteer experience.

Potential Volunteer: That would have to be when I was the Cub Scout leader for my son's Webelo Pack. We had a great time together. I did that for two years.

Interviewer: What was it about being a pack leader that was so much fun?

Potential Volunteer: Part of it was being with my son and having that time with him. And part of it is that kids that age are just great. Lots of energy and creativity, and sometimes they even listened to me.

Interviewer: It sounds like you enjoy being with children.

Potential Volunteer: I love it. I was going to be a teacher, but ended up not finishing college. In my last church I got to teach in Sunday school, too.

Interviewer: But Cub Scouts was your favorite volunteer experience. I'm wondering why it ranked higher than teaching Sunday school.

Potential Volunteer: I think it's because the person running our Sunday school was so strict with the children. I had a hard time thinking it was so important they memorize a verse each week, and that only the kids who did got treats. I didn't think that was fair to the kids who don't memorize well.

See how much more information was revealed by using an open-ended approach and linking questions than by firing off a series of closed-ended questions? And yet the discussion wasn't confrontational or stilted. That natural flow comes with practice—help your interviewers get plenty of it.

- *Use body language to make a connection.*

The vast majority of communication is nonverbal, so train interviewers to maintain comfortable eye-contact with potential volunteers, and physically demonstrate they're listening by sitting in an open, attentive pose.

There are many, many resources to assist you in training interviewers to be more effective listeners, but the most effective one may be a member of your church or community who's a professional counselor. Most counselors have highly developed listening skills and could help your team become competent in those skills listed above. Invite such a person to sit down with you and plan a training session or two, or to provide on-going coaching.

> "Your interviewers are *not* counselors."

A caution: Your interviewers are *not* counselors. They're not equipped to provide the care a trained counselor can provide. If you provide listening skills training, be clear about how to use those skills within the confines of the interview process.

The goal of an interview isn't to do therapy. It's to gather appropriate information to determine where to refer the volunteer, and to provide a listening ear. That's all. If something more is revealed and requires follow-up, train your interviewers in how to refer potential volunteers to a more qualified person.

A 90-minute training session is provided for you on page 85. It will increase the readiness of your volunteers to be effective listeners. You may also wish to have a training session to familiarize your interviewers with policies and procedures related to interviewing volunteers.

Develop Tools for Your Interviewers

Which tools you need depends on what process you use. I'd like to suggest a process for you to follow. It's one that's been used successfully in a variety of churches—large and small—and will be easy for you to adapt. It assumes you have trained interviewers, a system in place to capture and use information you gather, and people you can hand potential volunteers to for an additional interview and job offer.

This four-step process involves:

1. Sending a letter to confirm interviews you have scheduled (include with the letter a Discovering My Abilities, Skills, and Passions form that interviewees will complete prior to their interviews).

2. Conducting an interview using the Sample Interview Form as a guide.

3. Referring the potential volunteer to a ministry leader for a follow-up interview.

4. Confirming the placement was successful.

The tools you will need are the confirmation letter, the Discovering My Abilities, Skills, and Passions form, an Interview Form, and a follow-up letter.

And good news—there are samples of these forms for your use at the end of this volume! Let me walk you through the four steps . . .

Confirm the appointment.

Your marketing plan has been a success. People are interested in meeting with you or a member of your interview team to explore volunteering through the church.

It's helpful if potential volunteers give some thought to what they're good at doing before they arrive. They may be limiting their thinking about volunteering to only what they've done in church, and as a result eliminating their ability to serve in an area of ability, skill, or passion.

The Reach Out—Renew—Rejoice letter on page 106 is an invitation to think more holistically and to prepare for a personal interview. Send the letter and a copy of the Discovering My Abilities, Skills, and Passions form on page 108 to each person you will interview about a week before the scheduled interview. That's enough time to thoughtfully, prayerfully consider the questions, but not so much time that people set aside the letter and form.

You may choose to underscore the importance of thinking about the questions presented in the letter and form by calling the person a few days before the appointment to confirm the time and place, and to inquire if the letter and form arrived. Ask again that interviewees bring the completed form with them to their interviews.

There's a "hidden agenda" in making the confirmation call: It communicates that this is a serious appointment. Doctors' offices call to confirm appointments—you should, too.

Conduct the interview.

Here's where you and your team of interviewers put your training to use. God bless you as you bless others in your volunteer management ministry!

Refer the potential volunteer to a ministry leader for an additional interview.

Assuming no red flag arose to indicate the potential volunteer should *not* serve as a volunteer, you'll now recommend one or more ministries in which the interviewee could serve.

Please remember that *you will not offer the interviewee a position*. It's up to the person who will supervise the interviewee to bring the volunteer on board. You'll be in a position to show the interviewee job descriptions and suggest placement . . . but that's all.

The moment you want to reach is the one where you present ministry opportunities and ask, "Does this appeal to you?" What drives the opportunities you present isn't a list of open positions. Rather, it's which positions include abilities, talents, skills, and passions that align with those expressed by the interviewee.

The following chart summarizes how the interview process unfolds. It may be a handy tool to photocopy and place where you'll see it often.

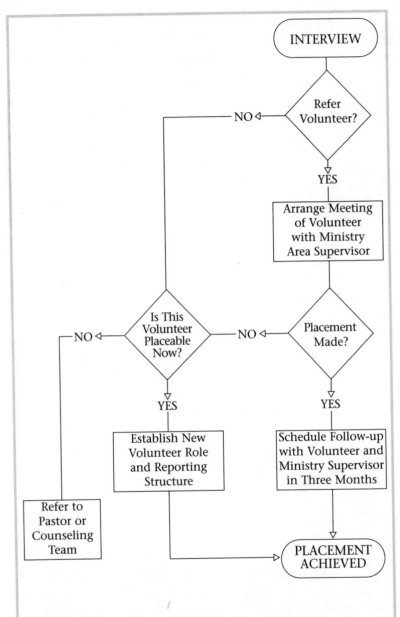

Confirm the placement was successful.

After suggesting a volunteer role for the interviewee, contact the person who supervises that position and ask him or her to schedule a follow-up interview with the person you or your team just interviewed. Then, a week later, follow up again with that supervisor to see if an appointment has been set.

It's this step where too often the ball is dropped and potential volunteers lose heart that there's a place for them to serve. Even if there's no current open position in the preschool ministry, if a potential volunteer expresses interest, the Preschool Director *must follow up promptly.* Timing is everything.

Also send the person you've interviewed a letter reminding him or her to expect a call for a follow-up interview. If a law enforcement screening will be required for the desired position, say so in the letter. Again, that's not something to hide.

Three months after the placement has been made, schedule a follow-up meeting or phone call with both the supervisor and the volunteer. Find out how things are going and whether the placement is working. Seek to resolve any misunderstandings and conflicts. If a volunteer isn't thriving in his or her volunteer role, go through the interview process again and provide another, more appropriate role.

There's another part of the volunteer placement that deserves a closer look: orientation. It's where you have the opportunity to ensure that volunteers get connected with the information and people they need to be successful.

You can't overestimate the need for outstanding volunteer orientation and training—and you'll learn how to provide them in the next volume of this Volunteer Leadership Series, *Volunteer Orientation and Training.*

FOUR
Active Listening Training Workshop

A 90-minute workship that will help you equip your team of interviewers.

In this hands-on workshop you will accomplish the following:

• Expose participants to five skills associated with active listening.

• Lead participants in practicing those five skills.

• Facilitate evaluation of participants in those five skills.

Supplies needed: Chairs, pens or pencils, a whiteboard or piece of posterboard and markers, one copy of the Active Listening Encouragement and Evaluation Sheet per participant (see end of this chapter), Bible, nametags.

Introduction

Welcome participants as they arrive. Even if you believe everyone knows the name of each other person, ask everyone to fill out a nametag as people arrive. On the nametag ask people to write their first and last name, and the name of a childhood pet, if they had a pet.

Encourage people to mingle and attempt to guess what sort of animal the other participants' pets were, based on the pets' names.

When the announced start time has arrived, gather participants together and say:

Welcome to this Active Listening Training Workshop. In the next 90 minutes we'll discover how the five skills associated with active listening can help us become better interviewers. We'll get a chance to practice those skills, too.

Let me admit right up front that all of us have room to grow in our listening skills—including me. This is a safe place to learn new things and to stumble a bit as we learn new things.

Open your Bible and read aloud 1 Peter 4:10, printed here for your convenience:

"Each one should use whatever gift he has received to serve others, faithfully administering God's grace in its various forms" (1 Peter 4:10).

Say: We can choose to become better interviewers for lots of reasons. It can be the challenge that intrigues us, or that getting better at this will help us professionally. It's a valuable skill. Maybe it's because we're the sort of people who, if we do something, want to do it with excellence.

Let me suggest this as a motivation: so we can cooperate with the purposes of God. It's clear in the passage I read and elsewhere in Scripture that each person in our church is designed by God to have a place in service. We're made to serve God in unique ways that we may not understand ourselves. The interviewing we'll do will help people find appropriate, rewarding places to serve. That makes what you do an important ministry!

And the skills you'll learn or have reinforced in this workshop are a big part of what will make you an effective interviewer.

Let's commit this time to God.

Lead in a prayer dedicating the workshop to God, and ask his blessing on your learning and application of what you're learning.

The Workshop

Say: Listening is more than just waiting for your turn to speak. It's more than a way to gather information. When we truly listen, we communicate warmth that allows interviewees to open up and share what—and who—they really are. We help the people we're interviewing feel worthy and respected.

Listening is a gift we give others.

In the next hour we'll identify and practice several techniques that help us actively listen to others. Active listening is simply this: listening to others, and letting them know we're listening. Sounds simple, doesn't it?

It's not. Most listening is passive, not active. The two types of listening differ in some important ways:

- *Active* listening requires us to be engaged and patient; passive listening demands nothing more than simply staying quiet.

- *Active* listening communicates concern, interest, and empathy; passive listening falls far short of that.

- *Active* listening often builds a relationship; passive listening usually doesn't.

- Finally, *active* listening is rare; passive listening isn't.

Turn to a partner and share about a time you talked with someone—maybe a friend or partner—and when you were done sharing, you felt truly heard. What was that like? You've got two minutes.

Allow two minutes, then call attention back to yourself by gently sounding a whistle or clapping.

Say: **Now share about a time when someone was hearing you, but not really listening. What was that like? Again, you've got two minutes.**

Allow two more minutes, then call attention back to yourself by gently sounding a whistle or clapping.

Say: **Quite a difference, wasn't there? Please call out a few words that describe how you felt when someone was** *truly* **listening to you—and let us know that. How did you** feel? Jot the descriptive words you hear on the whiteboard or piece of poster paper.

Say: **Now call out some words that describe how you felt when someone was not really listening. How did you feel?** Jot the descriptive words you hear on the whiteboard or piece of poster paper.

Say: **Here's what's sad: If we talked to the people who were with us in our second situations—where someone was with us but not hearing us—those people would probably say they *were* listening.**

Listening can be done well—or poorly. We're going to identify and practice some skills that make it likelier that someone we're interviewing will describe the experience with the *first* list of words.

Here's what we'll do: I'll briefly describe five active listening skills that we each need to master, then we'll get in teams and practice them. Please know that you don't need to become an expert in these to be effective. What you need is to listen to others in the way you want to be listened to; it's like the Golden Rule of Listening.

Here are the skills . . .

Skill #1: Help the interviewee feel comfortable.

Some of this is what you do physically. (Demonstrate as you continue.) For instance, be sure you place chairs so there's no barrier between you, but don't have chairs face-to-face—that's confrontational. Sit at a slight angle, so you can talk comfortably. Sit up straight, leaning slightly forward so you appear attentive and focused. Maintain eye contact that's comfortable, but not a stare-down. And minimize distractions by turning off your cell phone, and any radio or television that might snag your attention or the attention of the interviewee.

Also, speak in a pleasant, relaxed tone. Don't rush through your questions or speak loudly.

Skill #2: Communicate that you're listening.

React to what you're being told by nodding, raising your eyebrows, or responding in another nonverbal way

to the emotion and content you're hearing. The idea isn't to become a mime, but to provide clues that you're attentive and listening carefully.

Occasionally saying something like "I see" or "uh-huh" will provide verbal clues you're listening, too, but use them sparingly.

One great way to communicate you're listening is to use linking questions and provide an opportunity for the interviewee to elaborate.

Skill #3: Focus on what you're hearing.

Listening is *hard work*. It requires us to do things we don't normally do . . .

- *Keep an open mind.* It's hard to wait until the interviewee is finished talking before you decide if you agree or disagree, or form an opinion. We often listen just long enough to reach a conclusion, then express ourselves. The problem with this approach is that an interviewee may not know what she thinks about something until she's done sharing. And *we* certainly don't know. We must keep an open mind.

- *Focus only on the speaker.* Try to not think about what you're going to say next or about your own concerns. You can't be thinking about whether you rolled up your car windows and what an interviewee is saying at the same time.

- *Don't do too much sharing.* It may seem odd to say, but although you're trying to develop a relationship, it is usually counterproductive to disclose too much about yourself. The purpose of the interview isn't for you to share your volunteer experiences, but to draw out the interviewee. Disclose who you are, but only as it encourages the interviewee to share. If the interviewee asks you questions about yourself, respond—but redirect the interview back to the person being interviewed.

Skill #5: Reflect back what you hear.

This is perhaps the most difficult skill to master. You want to be able to reflect what you've heard by paraphrasing what you've been told. This allows you to know if you've listened accurately and to give interviewees the chance to correct you.

Here's what's tricky: You need to reflect *both* parts of the message you've received—the content and the emotion.

Here's an example of something you might hear from Mary when you're interviewing her: "When I was a volunteer at First Church, it was a good experience." (Deliver this line calmly and in a straightforward manner.)

Pretty straightforward, right? You might paraphrase that remark by saying, "Sounds like when you were at First Church you enjoyed being a volunteer."

Notice that my reflection paraphrase sums up both the *content* of what she said: she was a volunteer at First Church—and what I understood that she *felt* about being a volunteer: she *enjoyed* it. She never said she enjoyed it, she implied she enjoyed it. I put a word in her mouth to make sure I'm clear about how she felt.

If I was right, Mary may say, "Oh, yes, I loved getting together with the other volunteers and we became friends. I hope the same thing happens here." That's some valuable information about what motivates Mary to volunteer.

If I was wrong about how she felt, Mary will correct me. She might say, "No, I really hated it. It was good because it helped me be less shy, but I couldn't stand the people I was with." That's helpful to know, too!

Think of each message you receive as having two parts: content and emotion. Sometimes the content is really big and there's hardly any emotion. A lecture about cellular biology in science class is usually like that. The teacher sends you tons of content, but it isn't that emotional.

Other times a message has very little content, but lots of emotion. When you tell someone you want to marry "I love you" for the first time, there's not much content—but a *lot* of emotion.

When you reflect back to people what you're hearing, reflect both content and emotion. That can be tough because we're used to thinking we "get it" when people tell us things; that we don't have any cause to check if our assumptions are correct.

That's dangerous. Communication is so complex that it's amazing we ever understand each other at all. And where we misunderstand each other is often about how we feel. If you tell me your grandmother died, it means something very different if she was a big part of your life than if she was someone you'd never met who refused to see you. The content is the same, the emotion completely different.

So what happens if you reflect to someone that you think they're sad, when they're not? They're really angry, but they look sad.

Here's what happens: They correct you and move on. As long as your reflection is tentative, nonjudgmental, and it's obvious you want to understand, people don't hold it against you that you read them wrong. They straighten you out and move on.

How do you reflect? Here's a simple formula you can use until the process feels more natural and you can substitute wording of your own:

"Let me be sure I understand. You were a volunteer at your former church (there's the content) and you feel good about the experience (there's the emotion)."

And if you're stuck for a word that sums up the emotion, consider using one of these words: mad, sad, glad, or scared. They pretty much capture everything someone can feel.

See how challenging active listening can be? You need to listen not just to the words but also to the emotions. You have to focus. You try not to jump in or make judgments, and you want to encourage someone else to keep talking. It's hard!

Let's practice some of those skills right now. Believe it or not, it's fun—and you'll see huge improvement in your skills as you practice.

Form trios and ask the person in each trio who has the next birthday to be the Interviewer. The person with the next birthday will be the Interviewee. The last person in each trio will be the Observer. Trios will need to sit far enough apart from each other that conversations can happen easily, but it will be helpful if you can see each trio. That will help you signal stop times and let you see if a trio gets stuck.

Ask the Interviewer to arrange the chairs so they're angled and it's comfortable to talk. The Observer should sit off to one side where she can hear but won't be in the direct line of vision. Give the Observer a copy of the Active Listening Encouragement and Evaluation Sheet (found at the end of this chapter) and a pencil or pen. Tell participants they'll interview for eight minutes, but they don't need to watch the clock. You'll interrupt to call the session to a close. Encourage the Observer to take notes of times they see examples of what's on the sheet. And be specific—the more specific the feedback, the more helpful it is.

You'll have six rounds of interviews, and you need to provide topics that elicit both content and emotion but don't turn into deeper sessions than your trios are prepared to handle. Use one of these topics, or develop your own:

- Describe a family vacation from your youth.

- Describe a time from your childhood when you struggled in school.

- Describe a time in your life you were frightened.

- Describe a time you took on a challenge and were successful.

- Describe something you'd change about your house or apartment if you could.

- Describe something you'd do if you had 50 million dollars.

Once you've announced the topic and given the interviewee 30 seconds to think about it, start the interviews. Expect a lot of nervous laughter the first few times you have practice sessions; you're pulling people out of their comfort zones.

At the five-minute mark, blow a whistle gently or clap your hands. Ask everyone to take a deep breath, stretch their muscles, and then move the chairs so both the Interviewer and Interviewee face the Observer. Then ask the Observer to go through the Encouragement and Evaluation Sheet and give examples of what the Interviewer did well. The sheet also directs the Observer to ask the Interviewer and Interviewee how the process felt. Allow time for this discussion, then quickly move on.

Ask members of each trio to rotate chairs and do the exercise again with a new topic. Each member of the trio will have each role once. The way trios decide who goes next is up to them.

After you've participated in three interviews, tell participants they'll do another three interviews in round-robin fashion, with one change: Observers will now also take notes on how the Interviewer can improve. Instead of just encouragement, there will also be critique and evaluation. The goal will be to help Interviewers identify what skills they need to practice in the context of additional conversations at home or work.

You Should Be in Pictures

A Note: If you have the technology, or you are working with a very small group, another way to provide feedback is to videotape each session and include the Interviewer in viewing the tape. Nothing shows us more clearly how we're actually behaving than a video of ourselves. Interviewers will tend to see only their shortcomings, so be careful to be especially affirming.

After the second round of interviews, gather participants together. Ask participants how they feel about their practice sessions and how they'll put the five active learning skills to use elsewhere in their lives.

Suggest each participant take an Active Listening Encouragement and Evaluation Sheet home to keep handy. If you intend to hold another training or orientation session regarding procedures and policies, announce it at this point.

Active Listening Encouragement and Evaluation Sheet

As you observe the interview, make notes about the following interview skills. Your candid feedback will help the Interviewer grow in ministry effectiveness. Remember to be specific in your feedback and to offer compliments as well as critique.

Helps the Interviewee feel comfortable.
❏ Removes physical barriers to conversation.
❏ Sits up straight or leans slightly forward.
❏ Makes consistent eye contact.
❏ Speaks in pleasant, relaxed tone.
❏ Doesn't appear to be distracted or rushed.

Communicates listening.
❏ Is physically responsive with nods or facial movements.
❏ Provides sparing verbal cues.
❏ Uses open-ended questions.
❏ Uses linking questions.

Focuses on Interviewee.
❏ Displays nonjudgmental attitude.
❏ Displays patience.
❏ Appropriately self-disclosing.

Reflects back what Interviewee communicates.
❏ Paraphrases content.
❏ Paraphrases emotion.

After giving your feedback, ask both the Interviewer and Interviewee how they felt about the interview. What feedback does the Interviewee have for the Interviewer? What does the Interviewer think are his or her strengths . . . and weaknesses?

FIVE
Photocopiable Forms

Here's everything you need to launch your recruitment and interview campaign—from idea-generating marketing forms to follow-up letters to new volunteers.

Copy and adapt any of the forms you find here. They're yours for the taking, so long as you use them in your local church setting. Keep in mind that no form is truly a "one-size-fits-all" solution, so give serious thought to personalizing these forms for your unique situation. Ask someone in your church who has a writing background to work with you to tweak what you find here until it perfectly reflects your church's values and personality.

Defining the Purpose of Your Volunteer Ministry

Your Mission Statement:

Who does your volunteer ministry serve?

What services or products does your ministry provide to those you serve?

What is unique about your ministry?

Your Purpose Statement:

Checklist:

❑ Our statement of purpose clearly identifies why our volunteer ministry exists.

❑ The statement of purpose is inspiring to paid staff, volunteers, and clients.

❑ The statement of purpose provides clarity for decision-making.

Determining Your Target Audiences

Internal audiences:

What we *know* about these audiences:

What we *assume* about these audiences:

External audiences:

What we *know* about these audiences:

What we *assume* about these audiences:

Checklist:

❏ You've identified each audience your volunteer ministry needs to address.

❏ You've checked what you know against unbiased data (demographic information, church profiles, discussions with church leaders).

❏ You've checked what you assume with at least two members of each audience you've identified.

Setting Marketing Goals

Marketing campaign:_____

As a result of our marketing efforts, what do we want people to *know*?

How will we know we've accomplished this goal?

Who is primarily responsible for making this goal happen?

As a result of our marketing efforts, what do we want people to *believe*?

How will we know we've accomplished this goal?

Who is primarily responsible for making this goal happen?

As a result of our marketing efforts, what do we want people to *do*?

How will we know we've accomplished this goal?

Who is primarily responsible for making this goal happen?

Checklist:

❑ Be sure each goal is specific.

❑ Be sure each goal is challenging, but attainable.

❑ Be sure each goal is measurable.

❑ Be sure each goal is connected to a calendar date.

❑ Be sure each goal is connected to a person's name.

Volunteer Benefit Analysis Sheet

Marketing campaign: _____

Volunteer role being filled:_____

What benefits are likely to flow to volunteers who fill this position?

Skill set benefits:

Social benefits:

Knowledge benefits:

Emotional benefits:

Spiritual benefits:

Recognition benefits:

Checklist:

❑ Each benefit area has at least one benefit flowing from the job description for the role.

Note that if a benefit area is not represented, it may be perceived as a weakness by potential volunteers.

Marketing Message Delivery Planning Sheet

Synopsis of marketing content (*state in two or three sentences*):

Goal of campaign:

Target audience:

Proposed channels of communication (*How do you intend to deliver your campaign message to your target audience?*):

Resources available:

- Finances (*What's your budget?*):

- Time (*When do you need to finish? start?*):

- Influencers (*Champions who'll give testimonials or support*):

- Free forums (*Worship services, newsletters. . . Anything you can use without it impacting your budget?*):

Checklist:

❑ Be sure your plan is attainable using available resources.

❑ Be sure your plan focuses on the campaign goal and each part of your plan makes sense in light of the goal.

❑ Be sure you've identified a person who is responsible for each element of your plan.

Volunteer Ministries Placement Interviewer
Sample Job Description

Job Title: One-to-one Interviewer

Responsible to: Director of Volunteer Ministries and Volunteer Ministry Task Force

Desired Commitment: 6 months
4-6 interviews (approximately 30 minutes each), attend training session (2 hours) and follow-up meetings (2 hours)

Duties: Attend interview training workshop. Make appointments with those members you will interview. Conduct one-to-one interviews as assigned by Task Force. Fill out interview follow-up form after each interview. Feed appropriate information back to church staff or volunteer director. Attend follow-up meeting to provide feedback to task force regarding interview process.

Desired Qualifications: Ability to handle confidential information. Experience as a volunteer. Genuine, caring, "people person" attitude, and having an excited commitment to the concept of volunteer ministry.

Good listener.
Familiarity with church programs,
or willing to learn about those
programs.
Interviewing experience is helpful,
but not necessary.

Training: Interview training workshop is
                             provided and required.

Sample Interview Confirmation Letter

Reach Out—Renew—Rejoice!
"Each one should use whatever gift he has received to serve others, faithfully administering God's grace in its various forms."
(1 Peter 4:10)

Dear <u>Jack</u>:

Thank you for our conversation about the volunteer ministries available through <u>First Church</u>.

We place a high priority on involving members in appropriate, fulfilling ministry. We believe the Bible teaches that all of us are unique and important, and that we've each got something valuable to offer in service to others.

It would help me get to know you better if we could talk about some of the following things when we meet <u>on Saturday, July 26 at 2:00 P.M. in the church office</u> . . .

- What have you done that's given you the greatest satisfaction here at <u>First Church</u>? At another church? In the community?

- What have you always wished you could do?

- What do you enjoy doing in your leisure time?

- Is there a skill you wish you could learn or try?

- What are your hobbies?

- What do you feel you're good at? that you might be good at? that you're not good at?

- What have you done as a volunteer that you enjoyed the least?

And here's a question I'd love to explore with you . . .

- What would you like to see happen here at <u>First Church</u> that would have significance for you and/or your family?

That's a lot to think about, but we value your ideas, dreams, opinions, and suggestions. We welcome any questions or concerns you might have about the volunteer opportunities here at <u>First Church</u>.

I look forward to meeting with you, <u>Jack</u>. It's a visit with a wonderful purpose: As members in the body of Christ we'll be able to better know each other, support each other, and encourage each other in service to others and God.

Sincerely,

<u>Nancy Johnson</u>
<u>Director, Volunteer Ministries</u>
<u>First Church</u>

Discovering My Abilities, Skills, and Passions

Answer the following questions, while thinking of any area of your life that's currently exciting for you—church, career, home, family, school, your social life, leisure time, hobbies, or any other part of your life that energizes you.

1. Some things I believe I do well are:

2. Some things I think I'm not very good at are:

3. If given the chance, I think I might be good at:

4. One new thing I've tried recently that went well was:

5. Who encouraged me to do what I listed in #4? What made the person or persons think I could do it? Does this person or these people encourage me to try new things often?

6. Who are my mentors (my loyal, wise advisors) in life?

Sample Interview Form

First Church Interview Questionnaire

Name: _____ Spouse: _____

Home Phone: _____ Work Phone: _____

Cell Phone: _____ E-mail: _____

Address: _____

Birthdate:_____ Gender:_____ Marital status: _____

Church member since: _____ Is spouse member? _____

Children at home (*please list*) Birthdate   Church member?

Other children not at home, or family ties to <u>First Church.</u>

Have you served in any of the following capacities? (*please check*)

___ Church board or other congregational leadership

___ Christian education   ___ Youth ministry

___ Committee work   ___ Usher ministry

___ Other:

Where and when?

Leadership training received at church or work (*please explain*):

_____

_____

Other training received (*such as child abuse training, Stephen Ministries, and other training*):

_____

_____

Are there times of the day or week you are not available?

_____

Worship service you prefer to attend:

_____

Notes:

Permission for information to be entered into the church database (*please sign*):

_____   _____

Signature   Printed name

Today's date: _____   Interviewer: _____

Sample Interview Follow-Up Letter

Dear Jack,

Thanks so much for meeting with me and agreeing to consider being a volunteer in First Church's Preschool Christian Education Department.

That role is supervised by Karen Hedges.

Ms. Hedges will be contacting you by phone in the next week to arrange to meet with you to further explore your volunteering in that ministry. Though it appears that your God-given abilities, interests, and passions for service would be well-used in that ministry, it's a good idea to be sure. Additional discussion will help confirm our thinking.

Again—thank you, Jack. It's exciting to see you step out and serve. God will bless your efforts and help you grow as you serve others!

Though you'll be talking with Ms. Hedges, please call on me if at any time I can be of service to you.

Sincerely,

Nancy Johnson
Director, Volunteer Ministries
First Church